This book shows how we c
that portrays women as victii
wonderful, warm and eng.
that men and women can't make interventions about inequality
until we have had a conversation about the real barriers to gender
parity. She equips us with a practical framework for meaningful
action, enabling more of the difficult conversations that ultimately
allow the best people to advance by merit, regardless of gender.

**James Clarry, Chief Operating Officer,
Coutts and the Wealth Businesses of the NatWest Group**

Far too often, the finger of blame is pointed at women. We're told
we're not ambitious enough; we're not confident enough; we're
too emotional; we lack leadership skills. Here, at last, is a book
that aims to change the narrative and fix the system. Every boss
should have a copy.

Kate Bassett, Financial Times

Joy clearly articulates the benefits of diversity and the systemic
reasons it has proven elusive, but this book's power lies in its
tangible and practical solutions. Having removed the excuse of
ignorance, *Don't Fix Women* leaves you with only two choices: to
knowingly be part of the problem or part of the solution.

Nathan Coe, CEO, Auto Trader Group Plc

Advancing gender equality is not about fixing women, it's about
fixing some of the structural, cultural and societal expectations
that exist today. *Don't Fix Women* shows you how this can be
achieved in a powerful and practical way.

**Drew Gibson, Head of Inclusion,
Belonging & Wellbeing, Santander**

Our workplaces are guilty of creating and reinforcing gender inequality, structurally and culturally. *Don't Fix Women* is a practical and useful book with solutions on how to fix the problem; how to build inclusive leadership; how to transform workplace attitudes and values and how to address the obstacles that women face at work. Read this and be the change that's needed.

Professor Helen Pankhurst CBE

Joy is inspirational in her practical approach to creating a better, more gender balanced workplace. I have a twin sister and through my close relationship with her, have seen how she has not had the opportunities I have had, despite working in the same sector. While there are various initiatives focused on Boards and emerging talent, we should consider how much have we progressed over the past 20 years? Joy's book really challenges us to ask questions of our businesses and provides tools to equip us, and our colleagues, to be changemakers and to #breakthebias. A must-read, particularly for those in senior leadership.

Calum Brewster, CEO, Brown Shipley

Companies with strong gender diversity at all levels perform better. *Don't Fix Women* is mandatory reading for all leaders, helping them to understand the obstacles that women face within their businesses, drive forward conversations and implement solutions that improve women's representation within the workplace.

Fiona Dawson CBE, Chair of the UK Women's Business Council

An empowering route map for addressing gender equality in the boardroom. Advancing diversity and inclusion is an essential part of business and this book shows leaders how to create workplaces where women can flourish. A highly recommended action plan for all CEOs and those involved in progressing the gender agenda.

Fiona Hathorn, CEO, Women on Boards UK

My experience of working with an all-female team helped me to see the world through a different lens; it taught me so much and enriched me as a person. Joy's book resonates with me and gives men a great understanding of how best to support and develop women in the workplace. It is compulsory reading for all men who want to be the best allies they can be to women.

Mark Robinson OBE, Former Head Coach of England Women's Cricket

Don't Fix Women is an essential resource for business leaders and people managers looking to understand the gender equality landscape. It provides a framework for cultural change and practical actions for long overdue systemic changes to create a level playing field for ambitious women to thrive. If I was going to write a book, this is the book I would have written!

Denise Wilson OBE, Chief Executive, FTSE Women Leaders Review

Marking a much-needed end to the era of 'lean in' thinking, this book recognizes that women are not held back because of a lack of talent, dedication or drive, but because there are clear, structural barriers to progression in the workplace. Now is the time for all genders to read this excellent piece of work, and make their commitment to a more inclusive workplace.

Simon Gallow, Advocate and HeForShe Lead, UN Women UK

A refreshing and inspiring approach to accelerating gender equality in the workplace, *Don't Fix Women* is packed full of practical ideas and ways to move things forward. The section on menopause covers a wealth of compelling new material that I'd not thought about or read about before. A must-read for all leaders and managers.

Phil Burgess, Chief People Officer, C Space

Until now efforts to achieve gender parity have been focused on 'fixing the women', even though women aren't broken (and never have been). Now a wealth of statistical data and personal experiences have revealed the real problem, a broken system that operates on the principle that male traits and behaviours are superior to those of females. (Spoiler alert: they're not!) In this book, Joy Burnford gives practical guidance on how to remove the blinkers of the past and recognize actual talent and leadership for the future.

Tamara Box, Managing Partner EME, Reed Smith LLP

This book provides a comprehensive route map for organizations that want to create more equal and balanced workplaces for all. Women still face too many obstacles on their career journey – flexibility, caring responsibilities and menopause to name a few – and this book shines a light on what can be done to remove them. A must-read for HR professionals.

Victoria Winkler, Director of Professional Development, CIPD

This accessible book offers some great ideas for achieving effective progress in creating better gender balance at work and allows the reader to assess their own strengths and weaknesses as a gender diversity champion.

Frank Moxon, Senior Independent Director, Jersey Oil & Gas Plc and Past Master, Worshipful Company of International Bankers

Don't Fix Women will help leaders to change systems and cultures to level the playing field for everyone to thrive in workplaces of today. It is packed full of analysis, insights and actions and is a highly compelling and relevant read for anyone involved in addressing the challenge of gender equality at work.

Emma Rose, Chief Human Resources Officer, Travis Perkins Plc

This book won't disappoint. It is a clear and engaging read and tackles tricky subjects such as menopause, caring and monthlies in a way that will make business leaders think differently about gender equality in the future.

Vanessa Vallely OBE, Founder and CEO, WeAreTheCity and WeAreTechWomen

Listen up, CEOs! The answers are all here for gender equality in your workplace. Send every senior leader a copy with an invitation to join you at a summit to plan how you'll enact it.

Jessica Chivers, CEO, The Talent Keeper Specialists and Author of *Mothers Work!*

A practical how-to guide on how to build equal and inclusive workplaces. Joy brings essential insights, strategies and actionable advice on what we can all do to support women to thrive at work. This is an important book and compulsory reading for those who want to lead the way in accelerating gender equality.

Antony Cook, Partner, PwC

As a long-standing client of Joy's, Wickes has experienced first-hand how the tools and frameworks in this book can be put into action with meaningful results. This book will help move thinking on and transform attitudes to gender equality.

Sonia Astill, Chief People Officer, Wickes Group Plc

Extensively researched and informative, *Don't Fix Women* is a highly refreshing and valuable read. It is full of useful initiatives and ideas, large and small, to move forward and create the pathways to gender equality in the workplace. An essential resource for any HR professional and those who want to make a difference.

Caroline Bowes, Director, Human Resources EMEA, Dechert LLP

A brilliant, helpful guide for organizations which outlines the obstacles that women still face in the workplace, including the menopause. We are calling on all employers to sign the Menopause Workplace Pledge and this book demonstrates how to take positive action at work to make sure everyone going through the menopause is supported. Read this book to help make a change in your workplace.

Janet Lindsay, Chief Executive, Wellbeing of Women

As a gender equality partner, OVF is working with Joy and her team on the models and frameworks outlined in this book to progress its gender equality targets across the business and drive forward strategies to attract and retain women who want to progress into senior positions. A timely and insightful book, *Don't Fix Women* guides employers on how to adapt the culture of their organizations and reap the benefits of a more diverse and inclusive workforce. We have seen how this not only benefits the women, but it helps the men too.

Sian Prigg, Senior Learning and Talent Manager, Opel Vauxhall Finance

JOY BURNFORD

DON'T FIX WOMEN

The practical path to gender equality at work

With thanks for all your support!

Joy
xo

First published in Great Britain by Practical Inspiration Publishing, 2022

© Joy Burnford, 2022

The moral rights of the author have been asserted

ISBN   9781788603102 (print)
        9781788603096 (epub)
        9781788603089 (mobi)

Every effort has been made to trace copyright holders and to obtain their permission for the use of copyright material. The publisher apologizes for any errors or omissions and would be grateful if notified of any corrections that should be incorporated in future reprints or editions of this book.

Want to bulk-buy copies of this book for your team and colleagues? We can introduce case studies, customize the content and co-brand *Don't Fix Women* to suit your business's needs.

Please email info@practicalinspiration.com for more details.

Practical Inspiration
Publishing

MIX
Paper from
responsible sources
FSC
www.fsc.org   FSC® C013604

For Sally and Lucas
May your future have no barriers.

And with sincere thanks to Claire, for your
inspiration, motivation and dedication on my book journey.

*Gender balance isn't
a woman's problem
to fix. Fundamentally
it sits with the men.
Organizations need
to create the right
infrastructure for
women to thrive and not
just survive.*

*Gary Kibble, Chief Marketing Officer,
Wickes Group Plc*

Contents

Foreword

There is so much evidence on the business benefits of diversity, equity and inclusion, yet the loss of talented women at senior levels – and associated costs – still exists across all sectors of business. This is no longer about personal motivations founded on the future of daughters, this is about 50% of the population being recognized for their talent and creating a better, fairer working world for all.

Progress towards gender equality has been made but there is still a long way to go until women achieve gender parity at the very top of businesses. This is my aim for the next stage of the FTSE Women Leaders Review.

For decades, women have talked about juggling careers and home life and have so often watched the men they have worked with glide to the top unhindered. I liken the load that some women carry to rocks in a rucksack. These rocks can include a lack of opportunities, gender bias, caring responsibilities (both childcare and eldercare), menopause and a need for flexibility, which can all contribute to the unevenness of the playing field for internal promotion. Some of the rocks can be removed by women. Others need to be thrown out by a change in company practice and policy.

Societal norms, a lack of shared parental support and workplaces designed by men for men have exacerbated the problem. Sadly, this has left many ambitious women with little choice other than to leave corporate life or remain underemployed in more junior roles. This is not only frustrating for women, but also for businesses looking to increase profits, remain competitive and thrive in the war for talent.

So, why is it taking so long to make change happen? Tackling gender inequality as a mainstream issue in the boardroom has only really been addressed in the last decade or two. Earlier in my career it was often a hushed 'water cooler' conversation. Today, thankfully, more organizations are putting this firmly on their boardroom agenda, but it takes time for significant change to happen. Many business leaders are still uncertain whether and where to start and are looking for guidance on how to tackle this problem.

Many years of trying to 'fix' women have only slowed progress. Instead, we must 'fix' the organizations to ensure that every employee can reach their full potential. Only then can we start to change the outdated systems, structures and cultures that exist today. Now is the time for business leaders to have the confidence to step up, lead the change and leave a legacy for future generations.

In this book, Joy sets out a vision for reinventing workplaces and offers insights, explanations and practical solutions which show how organizations can make structural, systemic changes to reach gender equality in the workplace. It is an essential resource for you and all those in your organization with people management responsibility, helping you navigate your route towards a fairer, equitable workplace.

Denise Wilson OBE
Chief Executive, FTSE Women Leaders Review, a government-supported, independent initiative in the UK

A note on who this book is for

You may have picked up this book because you're looking for new ideas and inspiration on how to retain more women in your organization. You may be frustrated at the slow speed at which change is happening. You may know nothing about the subject and are simply curious about what you can do to play a part. Whatever your reason, this book explains the reasons why gender equality is not happening fast enough and what you can do to help move the dial faster.

By reading this you will become part of this change. Perhaps you're a director looking for insights and solutions, a human resources manager seeking guidance on how to make changes or an employee eager to learn how you can personally progress the agenda. Those with global responsibility for diversity, equity and inclusion should be mindful that recommendations may need to be adapted according to cultures, laws and working practices in different countries.

A note on diversity

There is plenty of research covering the various forms of diversity that exist in the workplace – for example gender, age, race, social class, sexual orientation and disability. My work is about gender equality in the workplace, and this book mainly examines the differing attitudes and actions in relation to men and women. As much as I would like to examine the full spectrum of genders (there are 58 different genders according to ABC News[1]), it wouldn't be possible in the space available to fully discuss these differences and so I have focused on women, and anyone who identifies as a woman, and the challenges they face.

While I may touch on other forms of diversity, they are not the focus for this book. Intersectionality (when other areas of diversity 'intersect' with gender) can compound the issue of gender equality. For example, a black, lesbian woman from a lower socio-economic background will undoubtedly have more challenges than a white, middle-class, degree-educated cis-female. One of the themes running through this book is personalization: by adapting your mindset to think about the individual rather than the collective, you will by default be supporting all minority groups and men as well.

A note on definitions

- ⊚ **Gender equality** is when all people, regardless of gender, enjoy equal rights, resources and opportunities.
- ⊚ **Gender equity** is fairness of treatment for men and women according to their respective needs. Equity recognizes difference and provides differential treatment to enable equal access.
- ⊚ **Gender parity** is when each gender is represented equally. It is often used as a metric to assess the state of gender equality within a group or organization (e.g., setting a target of 50:50 male/female ratio).
- ⊚ **Diversity, Equity and Inclusion**: In this book, I have mostly used the term D&I (Diversity and Inclusion) but the terms Diversity, Equity and Inclusion (DEI) and Diversity, Belonging, Equity and Inclusion (DBEI) are now also becoming part of the diversity dictionary.

Introduction

Definition of *fix*: 'Do the necessary work to improve or adapt something.'

'Haven't we done gender equality yet?' is a phrase that I hear bandied around as if it's a one-and-done, tick-box exercise. We are certainly not done yet! Sadly, we are getting further away from gender parity in the workplace. The World Economic Forum reported that in 2021 we were 268 years away from closing the gender gap in economic participation and opportunity, compared to 202 years in 2018. Despite some progress there is still a persistent lack of women in leadership positions, with women representing just 27% of all manager positions globally.[2] Furthermore, in the UK women account for only 5% of CEOs in FTSE 350 companies[3] and only 10% of the largest 150 companies have achieved gender parity on their board.[4]

The most significant issue for companies when it comes to gender equality is the leaky pipeline and retaining women (that they have already invested in), supporting their progression into more senior roles. One study predicts that every time a business replaces a salaried employee, it costs on average 6 to 9 months' salary.[5] For a female manager making £50,000 a year, that's a minimum of £25,000 in recruiting and training expenses. Other research suggests it can be even more – as much as twice the annual salary. Investing in your female talent pipeline at key life stages will reap rewards in the future.

Retaining women in leadership positions is also important to help attract talent: nearly two thirds of women look at the diversity of a potential employer's leadership team when deciding where to work.[6]

My 25 years in business informs my thinking for this book. This, combined with extensive research and interviews with hundreds of business leaders, CEOs, HR professionals, diversity and inclusion specialists and survey insights from thousands of businesswomen and men, has provided me with a rich data set from which to draw my conclusions. I am very thankful to the individuals who have collectively given me over 200 hours of their time for interviews for this book (see page 207).

Over the past ten years the UK government and the FTSE Women Leaders Review[7] have put pressure on the UK's largest companies to improve the representation of women on boards and in senior roles. And progress has been made. However, there is now a drive to shift focus to the appointment of women at the very highest levels of UK businesses, in positions such as CEO, Finance Director or Chair. A corporate-led initiative in the UK called 25x25,[8] with members and sponsors including BP, NatWest Group, Unilever, GSK and Morgan Stanley, has also set a directional target to achieve 25 women CEOs in the FTSE 100 by 2025 and 25% of the FTSE thereafter.

My research has provided overwhelming evidence that the answer to gender equality is not about fixing women, it's about doing the necessary work to improve an outdated system that wasn't designed for women to thrive. As Avivah Wittenberg-Cox and Alison Maitland say in their book *Why Women Mean Business*: 'Women don't need "fixing". Most of the attention and money given to this would be better spent on fixing the systemic issue of outmoded corporate attitudes and processes.'[9]

It's about men and women acting together as allies to support a cultural change in the workplace and the world, which will not only encourage greater gender equality, but will enable every single employee to be more fulfilled, more productive and happier.

Why is change not happening fast enough?

There are five things that I still see hindering progress:

1. Workplaces were designed by men, for men

The evidence shows that gender balance is good for business, but by taking time to look under the hood, you will see that the corporate machine was designed by men for men. We need to observe what causes the machine to stop working for women, so we can dismantle and rebuild an engine fit for the future; once you have designed your future vehicle, you will get where you are trying to go a lot faster. Centuries of male-dominated cultures, processes and policies need to be shaken up. I'm not blaming men here. It's a historical situation that has evolved over time and today, the priority is about levelling up the playing field. This is where those in a majority can start to create a ripple of change for future generations.

2. Gender pay gap reporting needs more teeth

The introduction of gender pay gap reporting in the UK has been a useful barometer for companies and has certainly raised awareness of the subject on board agenda. The gender pay gap for all employees in the UK was 15.4% in 2021, which highlights a fair way to go towards pay parity. There are still more women in lower paid roles than men – it is not to do with equal pay for equal work.[10] Despite being a useful benchmark to provide transparency it has been criticized as 'having no teeth'[11] as it doesn't mandate what employers with pay gaps need to do to address the problem. Effort now needs to be focused on really understanding what is holding women back and the obstacles they face, rather than trying to massage the data (for example, I have heard of companies recruiting more men into junior roles in order to balance up the numbers).

3. There is a confidence gap in leaders

Achieving gender equality in organizations is a tough nut to crack and one of the challenges is ensuring leaders have the confidence to know what to do. We need business leaders to feel confident enough to address and talk about this topic as much as other business issues.

It's often a challenging topic and it's a key competence that could benefit from more education in the workplace.

4. We need to start to shift societal expectations

There is a big cultural and societal shift that needs to take place in terms of how we value women's work and men's work and how the responsibility of childcare is handled and paid for. There is a lot we can learn from the Nordic countries who are leading the way here and recognizing a better balance in both the home and the workplace. Added to this, part-time and flexible working patterns like job sharing are often seen as low-paid jobs for women. Younger generations are now starting to make strides in shifting this attitude and hopefully these expectations will be consigned to the history books. This is something that we can all contribute to making change in.

5. There are too many obstacles on the path

During my research surveys with thousands of women, I have had the benefit of hearing first-hand about the obstacles that women face in their careers – fewer opportunities, lower pay, being in the minority, a lack of confidence in taking time out for maternity and childcare, to name a few. These challenges tend to build up for women as they go through their 20s and 30s (typically the time that women might want to start a family), which is one of the reasons women can fall off the corporate ladder before having the opportunity to reach more senior positions.

With all this in mind, what can we all do today to make change happen faster? It won't happen overnight and it takes a lot of persistence to maintain the energy and focus. But the key thing is to start today.

Why bother?

Gender is a business issue, not a women's issue. The case for gender balance in the workplace is overwhelming: a more culturally and cognitively diverse workforce makes good business sense. Let's put the moral imperative to one side for a moment and look at why gender equality is a business imperative (Figure 1). There is a clear competitive advantage for companies that get this right.

Figure 1: Why gender equality is a business imperative

$28 trillion added to global GDP
If women were to participate in the economy identically to men, they could add as much as $28 trillion or 26% to annual global GDP in 2025

25% more likely to have above-average profitability
Companies in the top quartile for gender diversity on executive teams are 25% more likely to have above-average profitability

3 X higher profit margins
FTSE 350 companies with more than 25% women on their Executive Committee have profit margins almost 3 times higher than those with all-male

£123 billion lost in pre-tax profits
An additional £123 billion in profits is on offer if companies with less than 33% women on their executive committee performed as well as those with 33% or more

61% of women look at diversity of employers
61% of women look at the diversity of the employer's leadership team when deciding where to work

19% higher innovation revenue
Companies with more diverse management teams have 19% higher revenues due to innovation

See Endnotes for references.

Where do I start?

So, you're sold on the idea that it's a good thing to do. Now you want some ideas and inspiration to make it happen.

My ambition is to inspire you to create a more equal and balanced workplace where every single individual can thrive. It is about fitting work around life rather than fitting life around work. It is not about women replacing men. It is about balance and the right person for the right job, but giving everyone the best and equal opportunity to be considered. And by doing this, productivity and profits will increase.

But there are still far too many obstacles on the path for women, and so this book shines a light on these so that you are clear about what you can do to help remove them.

> Women are as ambitious as men. Women are as bright as men. But if we ignore the systemic changes that are needed to eradicate bias in the workplace, women will not want to continue to bang their heads against a wall and so will leave.
>
> *Tamara Box, Managing Partner EME, Reed Smith LLP*

There is no right or wrong way to read this book. You can dip in and out or read from cover to cover. The book is divided into four parts:

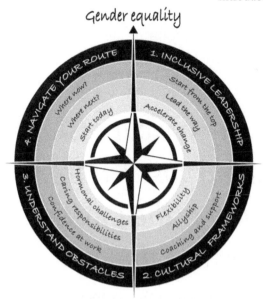

Part 1: Inclusive leadership – it all starts from the top.

Part 2: Cultural frameworks – changing the environment to enable women (and all employees) to thrive. Use these as your guiding principles around gender equality.

Part 3: Understanding the obstacles that women face at work – if you know what is blocking the path for women, and you have the cultural frameworks in place, you can work more easily to remove the obstacles in the way.

Part 4: Navigate your route – quick wins today can create a ripple for big change in the future.

Let's make change happen today

With the 'great resignation' at full tilt because of the pandemic, organizations need to adapt and change now, more than ever, to become the most attractive places to work.

While some organizations are further ahead than others, it will take persistence by everyone (and not just those in the minority) to make change happen. Change like this historically takes time, and yet we will all get there a lot faster if leaders of organizations recognize that even small shifts can make a big difference. I'd like to witness these ripples turning into big waves in my lifetime, or at least in my children's lifetime. This book will show you how. And, the best bit of all? It won't just benefit the women!

> *Having a clear vision and purpose led from the top is the most important thing to being a more gender-balanced organization, ensuring that senior leaders understand how imperative this is for business success.*

Drew Gibson, Head of Inclusion, Belonging & Wellbeing, Santander

Part 1

Inclusive leadership

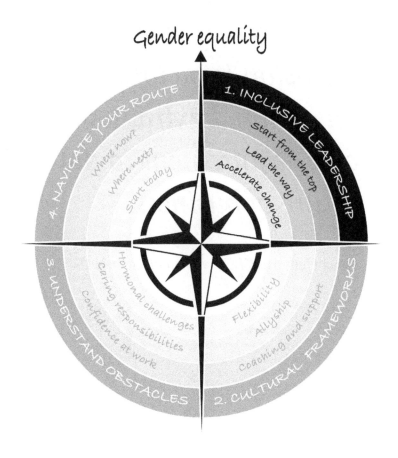

Gender equality

4. NAVIGATE YOUR ROUTE
- Where now?
- Where next?
- Start today

1. INCLUSIVE LEADERSHIP
- Start from the top
- Lead the way
- Accelerate change

3. UNDERSTAND OBSTACLES
- Hormonal challenges
- Caring responsibilities
- Confidence at work

2. CULTURAL FRAMEWORKS
- Flexibility
- Allyship
- Coaching and support

It is now undeniably clear that leaders must step up and that diversity and inclusion is no longer an optional extra, it's a core requirement to the future of business.

Fiona Hathorn, CEO, Women on Boards UK

Chapter 1

Adapting your leadership style for gender equality

This chapter explores:

- ◉ developing inclusive leadership through a lens of equality
- ◉ the PACE™ framework, which defines four behavioural traits of inclusive leaders
- ◉ how accelerating change requires leadership and commitment from the very top.

Start from the top

The world as we know it is changing at speed and in order to lead our organizations into the future, a different approach to leadership is needed. If you want to outperform your competitors and survive in the long term with a diverse workforce behind you, developing inclusive leadership through a lens of equality is key. Inclusive leaders are those who are aware of their own biases and privilege, seek out and consider different perspectives to inform their decision-making and collaborate effectively with others.

Women working in more inclusive cultures report higher levels of productivity, mental wellbeing and job satisfaction. A report by Deloitte of 5,000 working women, across ten countries, showed that only 4% indicated that their organizations have built inclusive, flexible and high-trust cultures that support women.[12]

PwC's 25th Annual Global CEO Survey also shows that only 11% of CEOs have targets relating to workforce gender representation. Interestingly, the most highly trusted companies are 1.4 times more likely to have gender diversity targets in their chief executive compensation plans.[13]

Emma Codd, Global Inclusion Leader at Deloitte, says: 'Meaningful and sustained change will only come when women experience "everyday" inclusive workplaces – whether virtual or in-person – where statements on the importance of gender equality are backed up by meaningful actions, and where goals are set and progress is measured.'[14]

The next section offers a fresh perspective on the behavioural traits you can hone or develop to become a more inclusive leader.

The qualities of effective leadership – already in a state of flux – have been changing more rapidly and obviously than before: being inclusive, connected, able to create a network of teams and to empower colleagues have all been necessary in a situation where no one could claim to know all the answers.

Baroness Morrissey DBE, Financier, Author, Campaigner[15]

Lead the way

My research and conversations with CEOs led me to develop a new framework called PACE™ which defines four behavioural traits of inclusive leaders: **P**assion, **A**ccountability, **C**uriosity and **E**mpathy, which are examined in more detail below.

Passion

Research by the Chartered Management Institute in the UK found that only 49% of employees said they have managers or senior leaders actively and visibly championing gender equality initiatives.[16] The organizations that are making strides with gender equality have visible, inclusive leaders who have a passion for change and are clear in their purpose. They have what I call *D&I in their DNA ('Diversity and Inclusion' in their DNA)*. This is not a criticism of those that aren't passionate – it is hard, but not impossible, to rewire your brain to change habits and biases that have been firmly wired in. It is possible, though, to become more aware of your own biases and be more purposeful in your day-to-day actions.

One CEO with a clear passion for gender equality is Nathan Coe of Auto Trader Group Plc. Auto Trader is listed in the Inclusive Companies Top 50 2021/2022 and has achieved its target to have 50:50 gender parity on its board. Nathan says: 'Without doubt, change requires passion, empowerment and a belief right from the very top of the organization to make the change happen and to call out behaviour or practice that is exclusionary. Too few at the top of organizations are talking passionately about this topic and yet we, as leaders, have a duty to ensure that women feel included and have the same access to careers that male colleagues have.'

So, if you are passionate about gender equality, you've got this. If this doesn't sound like you, or you don't yet have a clear purpose or vision for progressing gender equality in your organization, consider the legacy and longer-term impact you want to make in the world. What can you do today to move one step closer to this?

> When beliefs change about what's important or valuable, behaviours will follow.
>
> *Caroline Gosling, Director, Culture & Engagement, Rubica*

Accountability

Are you taking responsibility for diversity and inclusion in your organization? Leader-led accountability is vital for instigating change. If you devolve decision-making to others, you may find that you'll still be grappling with these issues in years to come. Think about how performance measures and mechanisms can be put in place to reward those who are taking accountability and demonstrating the right behaviours to drive change. David Dunckley, CEO at Grant Thornton UK LLP, explained to me that 'in order to hit gender targets, we have made sure that those making decisions are kept accountable via performance scorecards as this type of reward drives behaviour'.

> Setting the tone from the top, pushing for culture change, encouraging the CEO to lead from the front and to set targets, and holding management accountable are just some of the ways boards can have a positive impact.
>
> *Sharon Thorne, Global Chair, Deloitte*[17]

One person who takes accountability regarding equality seriously is Marc Benioff, Founder and co-CEO of Salesforce. In his book *Trailblazer*[18] he talks about a conversation with his 'employee success chief' Cindy Robbins, who asked him to commission a salary review for their 17,000 employees to see if men and women were being paid equally. Robbins was keen to ensure that this audit wasn't a 'hollow exercise'. She therefore asked him to commit upfront to acting on the results, no matter what it cost, to which he agreed. After this review, the cost to adjust everyone's salaries upwards was US$3 million. Had Benioff not been as committed and accountable to the change upfront, I wonder if he would have agreed to this expenditure? And this commitment to equality helped Salesforce reach the number one spot on *Fortune*'s list of the best companies to work for.

Here are four simple steps you can take to ensure that accountability around diversity, equity and inclusion is in place:

- ⊚ Set clear goals around diversity, equity and inclusion for all leaders, linked to performance measures and bonus payments.

- ⊚ Schedule regular meetings with your management team to review progress on D&I metrics and trends and improve where possible.

- ⊚ Make diversity a regular feature on executive committee and board agenda.

- ⊚ Communicate strategies, successes and areas for further work publicly and invite contributions for improvements.

Nikhil Rathi, CEO of the Financial Conduct Authority, made the point in a webinar hosted by Bayes Business School that 'you don't get rated as a top performer unless you're demonstrating behaviour that's consistent with our values, including our commitment to diversity and inclusion'.[19]

McKinsey & Company[20] also reported that nearly three quarters of companies believe that the work employees do to promote diversity and inclusion is critical, but less than one quarter are recognizing this work in formal evaluations (such as performance reviews).

Curiosity

What does being an inclusive leader mean to you? What does it mean to those around you? If you're not sure how you can support colleagues that are different from you, have courage and ask them how you can help. You need to foster a culture where it's acceptable to show vulnerability and admit that you don't have all the answers.

Learn to show vulnerability. Asking for help in difficulty is when you learn the most. Surround yourself with great people who you will listen to, who complement and challenge your style and your perspectives. That can be tough. You can want to be right the whole time, but if you are, you're either lucky or you're wrong and no one's telling you.

Fiona Dawson CBE, Chair of the UK Women's Business Council

Being curious is fundamental to the three cultural frameworks I outline in Part 2. Curiosity supports flexible working (so you can understand the individual needs of your people), allyship (so you can understand what it's like to be a woman in your organization) and coaching (asking questions is a key skill, along with listening).

Being curious and aware of your own biases and encouraging others to do the same is a fundamental part of being an inclusive leader. Open yourself up to feedback, listen and don't be too proud or defensive to make changes.

My biggest learning of being involved in BAME and gender networks is to be curious. This shed a light on my blind spots and things that I take for granted and has widened my view of the world and made me aware of the barriers and challenges that women can face in the workplace.

Gary Kibble, Chief Marketing Officer, Wickes Group Plc

Empathy

Empathy is one of the most valued managerial traits. In a study by the Chartered Management Institute,[21] 94% of those surveyed said that empathy was important and 50% considered it to be very important. Not only is empathy a key trait of being an inclusive leader, but those companies with leaders who listen to their people have lower employee attrition, less absence, higher customer satisfaction and higher productivity.[22]

In 2020 I ran a study entitled 'Rethinking leadership through a gender lens – new ways of working as a result of Covid-19'. It showed that a direct consequence of remote working was that organizations and people managers had a greater insight into the wider context of employees' lives outside of work. And a staggering 92% of those who had seen a change in their manager's leadership style said that the level of empathy and understanding had increased. The challenge we have moving into the future is ensuring that inclusive leadership traits, like empathy, are rewarded and encouraged.

Empathy is the opposite of ego. It is about truly understanding others around you, putting yourselves in their shoes, and where necessary allowing all emotions and difficult conversations to take place and become acceptable in a work context.

> I have no idea what it means to be a woman in this world because I am not a woman. But you can be open-minded enough to listen to what those challenges are. Recognize your own unconscious biases and do something about it. Influence the things you can influence and don't be the silent majority.
>
> *David Bailey, Chief Operating Officer, RBC Wealth Management*

Accelerate change

As well as the four traits above, urgency and prioritization are often the missing ingredients. Gender equality can often get de-prioritized when other more pressing matters take precedence. So, now let's look at how we can 'Pick up the PACE™'.

Urgently accelerating the greater inclusivity of all women within the workforce should not be left to women to sort out; this is an issue that men and women need to come together to action. And it requires leadership and commitment from the very top.

David Schwimmer, CEO of the London Stock Exchange Group, told me about a meeting some years ago, when he was asked how he felt about gender issues in the workplace and what plans there were for having more women in important leadership roles; his response emphasized his commitment to this and its importance, but he also acknowledged that it would take time.

He said he recalled the grimace on the woman's face in response to his statement. Now he sees that this is an issue that should have been addressed by organizations and society decades ago. 'In practice, change does take time and it has to be worked through, but it needs a sense of urgency at the same time. Careers have come and gone in the time we should have fixed these things,' he admitted.

It may also be necessary to make structural changes, rather than wait for things to happen organically through promotions. James Clarry, Chief Operating Officer of Coutts, explained to me that they 'needed to take every opportunity to create gender-balanced teams, with the skills needed for the future business, even if it means changing our structure to achieve this goal as quickly as possible'.

Without speed and urgency, our children will still be debating this in 20 years' time. My good friend and associate Helena Clayton reminded me of the popular Chinese proverb that says: 'The best time to plant a tree was 20 years ago. The second best time is now.' So, first check your own behaviours and then check the speed at which you want change to happen. If you didn't plant a tree 20 years ago, can you plant one today?

Don't be discouraged by diversity fatigue

It's sometimes hard to realize what's in it for you because you don't see instant rewards. You've got to want to do it, you must be able to do it and you must be prompted to do it.

Doug Field OBE, Joint CEO, East of England Co-op

A number of CEOs have told me of their frustrations with 'diversity fatigue', when actions that have been taken are not making an impact quickly enough. It does take time to make a difference and create an impact and people often get disillusioned because it doesn't happen quickly enough.

Collaborate with other leaders, share stories and examples of how you're moving the dial in your workplace. John Pettigrew, CEO of National Grid, told me about a coalition he is part of: 'Peer pressure is important when it comes to making real change. We have seen the group expand as other organizations realize the action they need to take.'

But to overcome the road bump of diversity fatigue, we must move quickly from tokenism to pragmatism.

Nobuko Kobayashi, EY Asia-Pacific Strategy Execution Leader[23]

By adapting your leadership style to be more inclusive, sprinkled with a sense of pace and urgency, you will not only be able to move the dial faster, but you will be role-modelling behaviours for others in your organization, becoming an ally to those who need you most and building a more profitable organization for the future.

Progress will not come about by forcing women to fit into the existing working environment. Instead, we need to accept the huge challenge of creating a new environment where men and women, from all walks of life, and every part of society, can thrive as individuals.

Amanda Blanc, Group CEO, Aviva Plc[24]

Part 2

Cultural frameworks

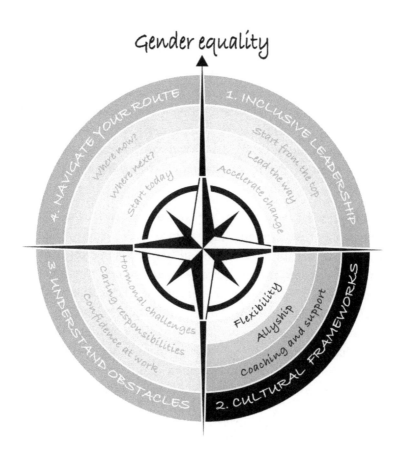

Gender equality

4. NAVIGATE YOUR ROUTE

1. INCLUSIVE LEADERSHIP

Where now?
Where next?
Start today

Start from the top
Lead the way
Accelerate change

3. UNDERSTAND OBSTACLES

Hormonal challenges
Caring responsibilities
Confidence at work

2. CULTURAL FRAMEWORKS

Flexibility
Allyship
Coaching and support

Preparing the ground for greater gender equality

Women are leaving, or thinking about leaving, their corporate careers in droves. The statistics are eye watering: one in three women considered downshifting their career or leaving the workforce in 2021.[25]

We know that gender equality is still a huge problem for organizations. We also know that having more women and a more diverse workforce has a clear benefit for the bottom line (see page xxi). So how can organizations make the shift towards more equal and inclusive businesses where everyone can thrive, regardless of their gender?

Advancing gender equality is not about 'fixing' women. Women are not the problem. Research has shown that women are perceived as being every bit as effective as men when it comes to leadership, and in fact are thought to be more effective in 84% of the leadership competencies most frequently measured (including taking initiative, acting with resilience, practising self-development, driving for results, and displaying high integrity and honesty).[26]

Women do not need fixing, but we do need to fix the cultural frameworks that currently hold women back in the workplace. The time is now for organizations to take action to create gender-balanced cultures for the future, where women can function, flourish, and most importantly, remain. As Maria Miller MP, the UK's former Minister for Women and Equality, says: 'Let's be honest, the workplace was designed by men, for men, and although times have changed, if we want women to achieve their full potential and enable them to contribute to our economic recovery we need to make sure the workplace is fully modernized.'[27]

Many leaders don't know where to start when it comes to 'fixing' the path to gender equality or removing the obstacles that women face at work. Others are more advanced in their thinking. I have spoken to hundreds of leaders – both male and female – about the issues they are facing and how they are advancing gender equality. What works or is right for one may not work or be right for all. No matter where you are on the journey, you can help prepare the ground for greater gender equality in your organization by embedding the following three cultural frameworks:

- ⊚ Flexibility
- ⊚ Allyship
- ⊚ Coaching and support.

These frameworks are designed to help you spot what needs to change in your organization, help you navigate your own practical path to retain and support women, educate others on the benefits of gender diversity, and create a culture of equality and inclusion that will have a cascading effect that benefits everyone.

> It's not about fixing women, but about giving everyone the springboard to be successful.
>
> *Justine Campbell, Managing Partner for Talent, EY*

We've convinced the naysayers that flexible working really works – and that people, and in particular women, are not at home shirking, but are working productively while still having the connection with home and family.

Ann Francke OBE, CEO, Chartered Management Institute UK

Chapter 2

Flexibility

This chapter explores:

- ⊚ flexibility through a gender lens
- ⊚ why a culture of flexibility is important and beneficial to everyone, not just women
- ⊚ the power of personalization within a flexible culture
- ⊚ job sharing as an underused flexible working option to support gender equality
- ⊚ the future of networking, its importance for women and how to make it more flexible and acceptable for everyone.

I believe the most important cultural framework to support a gender-balanced business is flexibility. Traditionally, one of the biggest challenges that mid-career women face at work is a lack of flexibility. Throughout my career I have witnessed many women drop out of the workforce for this very reason, or because they have been shoe-horned into a way of working that suits the organization and its prevailing culture. Damien Shieber, Head of Culture and Inclusion at Santander, agrees that flexible working is the answer: 'More flexible working will help close the gender pay gap and support parents and carers in balancing their responsibilities, both at work and at home.'[28] Not only will flexible working help to close the gender pay gap, it is proven to improve employee wellbeing[29] and productivity.[30]

I carried out research in 2019, which found a lack of flexible working was a significant barrier to women's career progression.[31] This barrier was removed almost overnight as a result of Covid-19, with both women and men equally experiencing the benefits of working from home and the flexibility this brought (despite the pandemic challenges). I hear so many stories of women who pushed for flexibility pre-pandemic and were told that it wouldn't work. We've now busted that myth and know that companies continue to achieve growth and profitability despite the move to more flexible working.

I carried out a subsequent study in 2020 to gauge the views and insights of women and men who had worked from home during Covid-19 lockdowns and found that 96% of respondents wanted to continue having the flexibility to work from home, 77% wanted the option to choose when to work at home and in the office, and 19% wanted to work from home all the time. The results were similar across genders, showing no difference in how respondents wanted to continue with flexible and remote working in the future.[32]

> Everyone is unique, but the obstacles people
> face are different depending on their gender,
> their race and their ethnicity.
>
> *Doug Field OBE, Joint CEO, East of
> England Co-op*

The pandemic showed us that big change can happen quickly when there is a mandate for it; organizations can use this opportunity to create a flexible framework for the future in which both women and men can work in a way that's good for them individually, while continuing to meet the needs of the organization.

Benefits of flexibility

Benefits for men

By experiencing the benefits of flexible working throughout the pandemic, men with partners and/or families have seen first-hand how this balance can enable them to fit life and work together with no detrimental effect on productivity. Many now have more time with their families and the ability to take on greater caring responsibilities and support their partners with their careers. Men that take shared parental leave typically have more empathy and understanding for the women in their lives who have taken maternity leave (either at work or at home). If more men do this, they can act as role models for others in their organizations and help to change the entrenched societal norms in the home too. So, the big question for me is, how do we encourage men to do this?

> It has come as a surprise that I have learned to love
> the new flexible approach that Covid-19 has given us.
> It has shown that it can be as productive as working
> in the office.
>
> *David Mash, Senior HR Business Partner, Wickes Group Plc*

A male friend told me that his company had insisted that he went back to working in his London office four days a week after the pandemic. He understands the benefit of in-person collaboration with colleagues but felt that three days in the office would be ample to make this work. In fact, two days per week is seen by leaders as sufficient time to be in the office to sustain company culture.[33] This change back to commuting not only impacts him – he enjoyed having time to spend with his daughter, rather than leaving home at 7.30am and not getting back until after 7.30pm – but his wife now, once again, defaults to being responsible for both school runs, which he was able to help with when working from home. The impact of this is that he is now looking for another job with more flexibility and his organization will lose a talented employee.

For many men, role-modelling change in the home is essential. For example, James Clarry, Chief Operating Officer at Coutts, told me about the ongoing conversations between him and his partner: 'Our desire is for our children to witness a mother as focused on her career as their father, and a father as committed to the household as their mother.'

Benefits for organizations

Retaining top talent

We all want and need some form of flexibility. By creating a flexible culture for the future, organizations will reap the rewards of retaining more women and men who need, or want, to work flexibly: for example, those shouldering the domestic and mental load at home, those who want to spend more time with their families, those that are dealing with health issues, men who want to support their partners to progress their careers, those who are responsible for eldercare or looking after a disabled relative, or indeed anyone struggling to get a healthier balance in their lives around work commitments.

As Edwina Dunn OBE, Founder of The Female Lead, says: 'Society has conditioned us to adopt an "unentitled mindset" whereby, for the privilege of rethinking working hours, women should forfeit promotion. They give up everything because they can't lose the flexibility they need.'

Increased productivity

The pandemic has shown that productivity increases when working from home. A survey by FlexJobs,[34] carried out during the pandemic, found that half (51%) of employees felt they were more productive working from home. Top reasons given for this level of increased productivity included fewer interruptions, more focused time, a quieter work environment, a more comfortable workplace and avoiding office politics.[35]

Happier, more engaged, trusted and motivated employees

Organizations that are aware of the needs of employees, and how and when they want to work, find they have a happier and more productive workforce, as well as increased gender balance in teams.

The truth is that everyone benefits from a culture of flexibility. We need to recognize individual difference, be more accommodating and offer a more personalized working profile, which we will look at in more detail now.

The power of personalization

> It's about personalization – asking and finding out what your people need and want at different times.
>
> *Nathan Coe, CEO, Auto Trader Group Plc*

While flexible and remote working are now more acceptable than ever, organizations must think carefully about how they communicate and provide the right structure to get the best from their people: how can this newly found flexibility be used as an opportunity to support a diverse workforce for the future?

Personalized flexibility is about recognizing that your people are all individuals, with differing needs at different stages of their lives. As Professor Rosie Campbell, Director at The Global Institute for Women's Leadership at King's College London, said to me: 'We must not assume that flexible working is good for carers and therefore by default good for women.' Anita Walters, HR Leader and Executive Coach at Aviva, also explains: 'You have to be careful about grouping people together – whether that is gender or different employee groups – as it is all about individuals and their circumstances, which are all different. Organizations shouldn't shy away from asking and having a conversation to find out what people think.'

Flexibility comes in many different forms, which is why a personalized approach to flexibility is important. Here are some different types of flexibility that can support a gender-balanced business:

- **Flexi-time:** employees choose when to start and end their work day or how long to take breaks for, within agreed limits.
- **Hybrid or home working:** some or all work done from home or another location.
- **Job sharing:** two people do one job and split the hours (the next section provides a spotlight on job sharing and how it can benefit a gender-balanced business).
- **Annualized hours:** employees have to work a certain number of hours over the year, but there is some flexibility about when this is.
- **Compressed hours:** such as working 36.5 hours over 4.5 days.
- **Four-day working week:** employees work a four-day week with no loss of pay in exchange for a commitment to maintain 100% productivity. The world's biggest trial of this new working pattern started in June 2022 with more than 3,300 workers at 70 UK companies.[36]
- **Shift swapping:** allowing a team member to request a colleague to work their shift.
- **Self-rostering:** employees can choose their work schedule.
- **Staggered hours:** an employee has different start, finish and break times from others.
- **Phased retirement:** reducing hours and working part-time.
- **Term-time working:** working a certain number of weeks per year to tie in with school term-time.
- **Part-time working:** working fewer hours than a full-time worker.
- **V-time:** employees can work fewer hours in exchange for voluntary reduced salary and benefits.

> You have to be careful about grouping people together – whether that is gender or different employee groups – as it is all about individuals and their circumstances, which are all different. Organizations shouldn't shy away from asking and having a conversation to find out what people think.
>
> *Anita Walters, HR Leader and Executive Coach, Aviva Plc*

PwC is one organization embracing flexibility:[37] it has committed to its 22,000 employees to continue with flexibility in the future based on 'two-way flexibility and trust', while making sure it meets the needs of teams, clients and the firm. This will include:

- An 'Empowered day' which gives its workforce more freedom to decide the most effective working pattern on any given day: for example, an earlier start and finish time.
- Flexibility to continue working from home as part of blended working, with an expectation that people will spend an average of 40–60% of their time co-located with colleagues, either in its offices or at client sites.
- Summer working hours for three months from June to August to reduce the working day on a Friday, with the assumption that most employees will finish at lunchtime having condensed their working week to allow the weekend to start earlier (with flex for employees who don't work Friday or can't flex that day).

> It's a shift in mindset. The importance of flexibility is high on millennials' agenda and we need to change.
>
> *Sarah Churchman OBE, Chief Inclusion, Community & Wellbeing Officer, PwC*

I have been fortunate to work in both corporates, small businesses and as an entrepreneur over the past 25 years. My corporate experience has been predominantly in the management consulting industry, and my experience of consulting firms is that they have been forward-looking in terms of flexibility. Consultants generally work where they need to get their work done, whether on a client site, a plane, a train, a coffee shop or a corporate HQ.

I have always adopted the philosophy of output-based working and have instilled this in the way I run my own organizations and teams. For me, true flexibility is being able to decide where you work, how you work and when you work, as long as you deliver agreed outcomes. I have employed a lot of women over the years, who love the freedom that a flexible way of working brings – many of whom have fallen off the corporate mountain for the reasons you will discover later in the book. I have employed people in different time zones, those with school term-time arrangements, those who want to work one day a week and many other combinations. I am a big believer in giving clear direction on what is expected of an individual and allowing them the freedom to deliver (usually above my expectations). It is also about knowing that one job doesn't have to be filled by just one person (see job sharing section). Managing a matrix of employees who work in different ways also brings with it more diversity of thought and experience.

The pandemic has shown us that great people can work from anywhere and in ways that work for them, because they tend to be performance led and output driven.

Claire Valoti, Vice President EMEA, Snap Inc

Personalized flexibility and this entrepreneurial style of working is one way to ensure that we create gender-balanced organizations for the future. Personalization is vital because everyone should be able to work in ways that suit them as an individual and their circumstances. This is clearly easier to do in office-based environments. Enforced flexibility for everyone is not the answer. We know from the pandemic that some younger people – those that live on their own and new joiners who require more support from colleagues – have suffered from enforced remote working. Some women may be desperate to return to work, while some men may be keen to keep the flexibility they've experienced, to give them more time at home with family and friends. Make sure you ask questions such as 'How can I help you do your best work this week?'.

The key is personalization; flexible working needs to be flexible.

Understanding individual commitments and challenges

> Our leaders feel a big responsibility to support our people's whole lives more than ever. It is not just about work anymore.
>
> *Georgina Collins, Global Chief Talent Officer, Interbrand*

I chatted to Sonia Astill, Chief People Officer at Wickes Group Plc, while she was home-schooling her two boys during the pandemic about how she managed this time with her team. All team members shared what hours they needed to be available for other commitments (mainly home-schooling at this point!) and then as a team they worked out a system for when and how they could each work, ensuring there were common times that they could come together for team meetings and collaboration. They made sure they honoured the times that their team members were unavailable. This level of collaboration ensured that there was appropriate and personalized flexibility within the team. It wasn't always easy, but by communicating regularly about what was working and what wasn't, it worked.

One other client told me that they had put in place 'non-negotiables' so that every team member had the chance to put key things in their diary – whether it was a school pick-up, yoga class or a dog walk. Everyone respected these and by discussing each team member's 'non-negotiables' upfront, a culture of flexibility was created without the stigma that can be associated with people leaving the office early.

Top tips on personalization

- Remember the key to successful flexible working is personalization and treating your people as individuals. Enforced flexibility for everyone is not the answer.
- Empower employees, where possible, to decide how, when and where they work. Trust your people. Let them decide how they can structure their days to suit them and have successful engagement with their team.
- For office-based work, measure and reward performance on output and an employee's ability to get work done on time and done well, rather than on hours spent.
- Ensure every employee knows what is expected of them and how their performance will be evaluated.
- Recognize that an employee's situation can change over time and over their career. Flexible working might be needed at stages of an employee's career, but not throughout.

> @ Encourage managers and those in senior positions to role-model flexible working behaviours from the top to avoid a culture of presenteeism and e-presenteeism. This will set the standard for what is acceptable or not.
>
> @ Consider asking team members to share their 'non-negotiables' and times they need to be available for other commitments so that appropriate times for team meetings and collaboration can be put in place.

Now we have looked at personalization, the next section shines a light on a particular flexible working option that is still underused but, if implemented well, can be a great tool for improving gender equality at work.

A spotlight on job sharing

Job sharing is a flexible working option which needs more recognition as a tool to retain women in the workplace. If done well, it allows individuals (both women and men) to progress their careers alongside family and other commitments and helps to shift some of the entrenched societal and cultural expectations that men are the breadwinners and women are the caregivers.

One reason job sharing is in this book is thanks to Will McDonald, former Group Sustainability and Public Policy Director at Aviva Plc. I heard him speak at an event, where he described how he and his job-share partner were the only known male senior job share they had come across in the whole of the UK. I couldn't quite believe it. All I could think about was how job sharing (by men or women) in senior roles could support gender equality and women's careers – either by senior level staff doing a job share, or by their spouse or partner doing a job share.

I am surprised that job shares in senior roles are not more common. Although there can be some obstacles, which I cover below, there are also a whole host of benefits, especially now organizations are thinking more flexibly about how and when work is being done. If the pandemic has taught us anything about the way we work, it's that we can make big change happen if there is enough of a mandate behind it.

It's time we move our thinking from 'it's too difficult' and 'it can't possibly work for my organization or role' to 'anything's possible if we learn from those that have been successful in making it happen'. Plenty of people thought that working from home was too difficult and couldn't be done. Let's not wait for another pandemic to make us think about how things like job sharing can work.

What do we mean by job sharing?

Job sharing – a term that was coined in the 1960s – is when two employees share the responsibilities and duties of one full-time job, with pay, benefits and holiday being split pro-rata. Roles can be split in any number of ways: for example, one person might work Monday to Wednesday and the other work Wednesday to Friday, or some job shares work in the mornings and the other in the afternoons, while some work alternate weeks.

When it comes to senior roles, job sharing has not been as popular as other forms of flexible working. However, the picture is beginning to change, and more organizations are seeing the benefits of job sharing for all (and not just for those with caring responsibilities) to address the gender gap in senior roles. Out of the 2,731 people registered on the UK's Civil Service Job Share Finder, 20% are now men. This is double what it was when it launched in 2015.[38]

In its most basic form, job sharing can be great for both men and women who want to continue their career part-time, while maintaining other commitments, caring responsibilities, or a role at home. It can also enable their partners to focus on their own careers.

A great start is to learn from others who have made job sharing work to see how both organizations and the individuals involved can benefit. Below is an extract from a conversation that I had with Will McDonald about his role at Aviva and how it all started.

Case study: Will McDonald, Former Group Sustainability and Public Policy Director at Aviva Plc and Chair of Trustees at The Fatherhood Institute

Where did the idea for a job share come from?

There were two things that prompted a job share conversation for me. First, I had been working part time for four days a week. This was good but rather unsatisfactory. I didn't work on Fridays, so spent most of my Mondays working out what I had missed on Friday! Second, my wife and I had the intention to be equal both at home and at work and didn't want to fall in the trap society lays for you in heavily gendered roles.

When a colleague went on maternity leave, I considered whether I might approach her and see if she would be interested in a job share on her return. When I mentioned the idea to my boss, Sam White, he said that *he* would really like to do a job share with me. This was the best of both worlds – I got a promotion and a pay rise at the same time as reducing my hours. It was a 'warm' job share as I had covered his job for about a year when he went on parental leave, and we knew each other's roles inside out.

How did you convince Aviva that the job share was a good idea?

There were three things that we did that helped to persuade them to let us give the job share a go:

We promised we would do it for a six-month trial, at which point anyone could call it off.

We produced a short paper based on conversations with eight job share pairs and their thoughts and insights on how it worked to demonstrate that we were taking it seriously. The findings covered things like trust, communications, managing a team, managing stakeholders, even details like setting out-of-office messages and whether the people we spoke to enjoyed job sharing. Every single person was evangelical about the concept.

We drew up a set of principles on how we would operate. This not only helped to clarify how things would work between us, but it also showed the company what we were going to do to make this a success and that we still had great ambition for our role.

What do you do with the two days you're not at work?

When I started my job share I had full days with our youngest who wasn't yet at nursery. It was brilliant, and a real eye opener in showing me how parenting can be incredible but also relentless. I did enjoy it though. That experience made me a better parent. I always say that women are not necessarily better at childcare, but they do more of it and men generally don't practise enough to improve.

Now my kids are at school, when I'm not at work I volunteer for the National Trust as a ranger, and I have also completed a Master's in conservation management by distance learning over two years, neither of which I could have done without the job share.

What makes the job share relationship work?

There is one piece of advice I would give: you must trust each other, but you don't have to like each other! Sam (my job share) and I go away two to three times a year to discuss how we are both feeling about the role, whether we are enjoying it, where we are heading in the future etc. It's a bit like a work marriage.

Do you think you have started a new trend?

I am perpetually disappointed at the lack of men doing job shares. There are a number of mixed gender or all female job shares, but we are the only all male job share we have come across in the UK. I think it will happen, but slowly. As more men are involved with their kids' upbringing, they realize that the demands of work are incompatible with this after parental leave.

The main reaction we get from other men is 'great idea, but it wouldn't work for my job'. We don't split the job at all and we have probably achieved more together than alone. Both of us do all parts of the job and it is split by time, not task. If you don't do this, it ends up being two people doing part-time roles. We also have a great PA, which helps.

How flexible is job sharing?

There is huge flexibility built into a job share. There is clearly an extra cost to the company, as they are paying for six days rather than five, but the benefits more than make up for that. When I went off for seven months when I was ill, Sam stepped up the very next day and went full time. Similarly, when he went on parental leave with his second child, I went full time. There were no recruitment or onboarding costs to manage, and our teams didn't have to learn to work for someone new. I am also very lucky I can make my life work on a three-day salary.

Why is job sharing the exception rather than the rule?

Given the benefits that Will describes in this case study, why is job sharing the exception rather than the rule? There are pockets in industry where job sharing seems to be considered more acceptable. The Civil Service has been offering job sharing for many years, and in other industries job sharing has been more prevalent in the lower salary levels and administrative functions for women. However, it is still the exception to find senior level job shares.

It is easy to think that job sharing is simply for women who want to accommodate more childcare and domestic responsibilities. Researching this book has opened my eyes to how job sharing can benefit everyone, not just parents.

How to overcome obstacles to benefit all

Let's start by looking at some of the reasons that have been given as arguments against job sharing. I have summarized these as the four Cs:

- ⊚ **Cost** – we'd end up paying more for a job share than a single full-time role.
- ⊚ **Culture** – it's not the way we've done things around here.
- ⊚ **Comprehension** – we're not sure how we could make it work (e.g., measuring performance), especially in more senior roles.
- ⊚ **Competition** – we'd worry about egos at play.

By addressing each of these, both organizations and individuals can reap the benefits and rewards that job sharing can bring.

Cost

We operate in a world where jobs are complicated and need a variety of skills. Job shares enable organizations to gain twice as many skills, twice as much knowledge and twice as much talent and experience, which more than justifies the additional cost. Job shares also provide:

◎ **Continuous job coverage:** If one job share partner goes on sick leave, holiday or even leaves the organization, you won't ever be left without someone in the role. It is also useful for partial or phased retirement.

◎ **The advantage of less managerial input:** Job shares typically need less direction as individuals as they can support, coach and give feedback to each other, and keep each other accountable.

◎ **Greater retention of staff:** Job sharing gives individuals greater control of their personal and professional lives, thereby increasing retention rates and reducing the cost of staff turnover.

As Karen Mattinson, Co-founder of flexible working consultancy Timewise, says: 'You shouldn't get hung up on how many days each person does, or the cost: 1.2 times the cost doesn't matter if you are getting 1.5 times the output. It's about designing jobs for maximum business impact.'[39]

Culture

Men are more likely to discriminate against flexible workers, while women, especially mothers, are more likely to suffer from discrimination.[40] It is important to educate everyone about the benefits of job sharing and flexible working. And a job share between different genders could be one way to bring gender balance to the organization! Job sharing can become normalized as part of a more flexible working culture by:

◎ **Advertising all jobs as potential job shares:** If organizations advertised jobs as potential job shares and had the frameworks and resources in place for it to be the norm, all roles could potentially be filled by job sharers. I am not saying that all jobs must be job shares – it's about offering the flexibility where you can. This is particularly useful when it comes to mid-career roles.

◎ **Prioritizing wellbeing:** Wellbeing is such a big topic resulting from the pandemic – I don't know many organizations that aren't prioritizing the wellbeing of their employees or looking for ways to support their people. Job sharing is a great vehicle for allowing employees to balance work and other commitments, whether this is childcare, eldercare, further education, voluntary work, hobbies or even just more time to relax!

◎ **Making job shares part of the conversation:** Make sure your HR team and managers know that job sharing is an option they can raise with anyone keen for more flexibility. Once there are examples of job shares within the business, these can be used as role models and employees are likely to feel more confident suggesting and exploring the possibility for themselves.

Comprehension

One of the most common obstacles employees may face is reluctance from their employer to road-test ways of working that haven't existed before. Job sharing, certainly at senior levels, has not been prevalent, but by understanding the benefits (even just by reading this book), you will be armed with the ammunition needed for change. Case studies are effective to demonstrate what is possible – whether that is reaching out to anyone you know who has tried it or asking your network if they have job shares within their business; being able to show examples of how successful job sharing can be in practice can be a great motivator to put it higher on the agenda.

Benefits to businesses include:

◎ **More productivity:** Two individuals working together will tend to be more ambitious and have the confidence to do greater things. Leadership can be lonely, and it can really help to have someone else to collaborate and bounce ideas around with.

◎ **Attracting staff and increasing a diverse talent pool:** Flexible working arrangements can increase job applications by 30%.[41]

◎ **Learning and development**: One of the key benefits is that job share partners can learn from each other, resolve challenges together and can create on-the-job coaching and development.

> We can talk through tricky decisions, get confidence from one another and make use of both of our skills. I have actually found it makes me more ambitious in my career, knowing I have a way to balance out work.
>
> *Ian Shepherd, Director of Trade Policy in the Department for International Trade (in a job share with Jenny Ashby)*[42]

Competition

Of course, you must be careful about how job share partners are matched and when pairing individuals you need to consider personalities and fit. Consider if there is a risk of clashes in ways of working, which can lead to competition rather than collaboration. However, if time is spent at the outset agreeing collective responsibilities, outcomes and how both work and successes will be shared then it will encourage a 'We versus I' mindset – one of the key ingredients to making a job share successful. Employing a coach can be useful here to bring in an external perspective and help align what success looks like.

Job sharing in practice

This second case study is an example of a successful job share and how, if done well, it can be a useful tool in addressing the recruitment and retention of senior women. It is from a conversation with Charlotte Cherry and Alix Ainsley at the John Lewis Partnership. They talked to me about how job sharing has helped them to balance their careers with motherhood, as well as progress their careers in ways that wouldn't have been possible if they'd worked alone.

Case study: Charlotte Cherry and Alix Ainsley, Director of Talent & Learning, John Lewis Partnership

Alix Ainsley and Charlotte Cherry embarked on their first job share at GE in 2013, having previously worked separately within the company. In 2016 they accepted the roles of HR Director at Lloyds Banking Group, in their first external appointment as a job share. They have moved as a team from Lloyds to Dyson, Quilter Plc and now the John Lewis Partnership. Alix and Charlotte first approached job sharing to achieve better balance between work and their young families (both have two children).

How has job sharing helped you to have flexibility in your life and work?

Alix: When I was full time, I didn't make the best choices for me and my family. In order to deliver at work, the balls I dropped tended to be those around my own wellbeing or prevented me from having the right connections at home. The job share forces a firebreak for two days each week to let go of work and be present at home.

Charlotte: We often see women checking out of their careers early because they just see the sacrifices they will have to make between family and work. Sharing responsibility at work, and at home if you can, certainly reduces the sacrifices you have to make. Both of our husbands work flexibly, which means we have equality in the home and we share more of the domestic chores which definitely helps when navigating a senior role.

How has the job share impacted your career progression?

Alix: Confidence can be such a big barrier to career progression and taking on new challenges. Having a partner in crime can really help to keep you strong and go for opportunities you might not otherwise go for. A lot of people think that job sharing is about stepping back not stepping up. For me, the job share has been a career accelerator and has propelled me in my career. A lack of confidence would definitely have held me back if I'd been doing it solo.

Charlotte: I remember someone asking me when I was going to be ready to go back to full-time work so that my career could accelerate. Comments like this stick, which is why I'm passionate about role-modelling job sharing as a tool for advancement, not for stepping back.

How do you think job shares benefit businesses?

Charlotte: Leadership can be lonely and often support feels less accessible. Sharing your role can help with this and, I believe, is a missed opportunity for businesses. There's something unique about sharing the accountability that makes it far less lonely.

Are there downsides?

Alix: You often have to pedal twice as hard to make it work. That's the burden that comes with job sharing. We put a lot of investment into the fluidity of our handover. Sometimes we need to talk things through, and this may happen on a Sunday night, for example. However, in a senior role, this isn't unusual, and you acknowledge that you might have to pick things up out of hours.

What is your advice for anyone considering a job share?

Alix: If you have people that are considering a job share, find out what the motivation is behind it. If they're doing it because they want to step back and take on less responsibility, it won't work. It's hard work and not for the faint-hearted! This is why it complements career acceleration.

Why do you think job sharing is not more common?

Charlotte: Until you see it working in practice, you assume all sorts of myths and legends. How do you manage two people? How do you lead a team? Doesn't it confuse customers? We have demonstrated the value and tend to leave a trail of new job shares wherever we work. Even though we enjoy it, it makes me a little sad that we are still called out as trailblazers for senior job sharing and that we are still a bit of an anomaly in organizations. It should be far more normal.

Why should HR teams be supporting more job shares?

Charlotte: How to retain and attract a diverse workforce should be on the agenda of every HR director, so why wouldn't you consider job sharing as a tool for creating diverse thinking in your leadership teams? And this is not just something for women. Men are at a point too where they want to work in different ways. There are many applications for job sharing – for example, we know it has been used as a tool to mitigate challenges around succession planning and as a retirement aid.

Top tips for job sharing

- Advertise all roles as potential job shares. Applying to do a role as a job share or changing a role to a job share typically seems to involve the parties in question having to build a business case for it. This is where organizations can get smarter. Job sharing can become normalized as part of a more flexible working culture.
- Be proactive. There will be men and women working five days a week who want to be part-time, or women who may want to work part-time when returning from maternity leave. Always offer job sharing as an option to try to prevent a resignation.
- Make sure individual and joint responsibilities are clear at the outset and ensure there is a shared vision between parties for the role. There needs to be a good understanding of the job share business plan and contractual agreements – who is responsible for what and managing performance.
- Have clarity around the process for performance reviews and when job sharers are treated as individuals and when they are treated jointly.

> ⊚ When things go well, give job sharers praise and joint credit for things, as well as when there are areas for improvement – you win together, you lose together.
>
> ⊚ Keep an eye out for the chemistry and fit of the individuals involved. Avoid a clash of egos which could potentially lead to competition rather than collaboration.
>
> ⊚ Give job share partners the time for off-site thinking days (quarterly works well) to assess strategy and effectiveness of role against objectives.

Flexible networking for the future

In the same way that Covid-19 has given us a chance to rethink ways of working, now is also the time to rethink networking and create a framework where people are given the opportunity to interact and make valuable connections with others in a more flexible way.

So, why is networking so important for women and for progressing gender equality? What does the future of networking look like? And most importantly, how can we rethink networking that works better for everyone? Time is short and precious. Networking, more than ever, needs a clear purpose, personalization and plan for when it takes place. There are many ways of creating great networking opportunities that aren't just mingling over a glass of wine after work is over.

Why networking is so important for women

Networking is fundamental to career progression for everyone, not just women: we've all heard the saying, 'It's not what you know, it's who you know'. More than three quarters of all jobs are filled via networking[43] and those who interact with senior leaders on a regular basis are more likely to ask for and receive promotions, remain within their organization and aspire to reach the top. Many women I've met in my career are excellent networkers, but networks don't work in the same way for them as they do for men. Networking to achieve gender balance needs rethinking.

Unfortunately, women get less access to senior leaders than men,[44] which is a real concern for gender equality when you consider that networking builds relationships and genuine connections, so that:

- conversations can happen more freely and in less formal situations
- it is easier to find mentors and sponsors
- you can find out about career opportunities
- you can ask for help from your new connections more easily in the future.

However, many people hate the idea of networking. Pressing the flesh. Working the room. Some people even find that professional networking can make them feel dirty![45] I am someone who really loves networking, and even I feel daunted by walking into a room when I don't know anyone – I dread to think how those who really don't enjoy it must feel.

But it doesn't have to be this way. A personalized and inclusive networking strategy will enable everyone in your organization to thrive, whether they are an introvert or extrovert.

Think of why the so-called 'old boys' network' works for men: by meeting in an environment where men feel comfortable and can talk about shared interests, they build up relationships so that when someone wants a favour or a step-up, (a) they are the first people they think of, and (b) they are happy to put them forward as they understand that person as an individual. By creating opportunities where everyone is in the same place, hierarchies are broken down. Networking is a chance to create business relationships and, when opportunities arise, you are more likely to remember someone you have met and had a shared experience with.

Ultimately, if women are not given the opportunities to network, or given the right environment to network, they are deprived of the ability to build up their contacts, to be more visible, and to progress in their careers on a level playing field with men.

But this is not about creating women's networks. Yes, there is a place for female-only and male-only networking as spaces to gain support, share experiences, and get help or inspiration. Women's networking groups have traditionally been a positive force for personal development, advocacy and focus on how to bring about change and achieve equality and equity in the workplace. They can also be a great way of supporting and empowering women at work, and a place to talk about the issues that affect them most, particularly around the obstacles they face on the path to leadership, which are covered in Part 3 (including hormonal challenges, caring responsibilities and confidence at work).

However, the problem comes when there is no collective network and the 'men's network' and the 'women's network' only meet up individually – you miss out on the cross-fertilization of ideas and learning from each other, and women can potentially miss out on access to senior leaders. A more inclusive approach to networking gives those in a minority a sense of belonging with the majority, where the power of leadership typically lies.

Again, it's all about personalization

It is critical to remember that networking means different things to different people. It does not have to be an evening cocktail party or a day at the golf course. One definition of networking is 'the action or process of interacting with others to exchange information and develop professional or social contacts'.[46] Organizations can create a framework to allow this exchange to happen at every level, whatever preferences and circumstances individuals have. If we change the idea from 'working the room' to 'understanding and being of service', then we enable all individuals to build and develop new business relationships that will flourish for the benefit of both the individuals and the organization.

There are many ways that organizations can set up networking opportunities and they don't have to be what we might traditionally associate with networking. Activities can be designed to suit every individual; it is not one size fits all. All employees will benefit from networking, but don't make assumptions that everyone wants to network in the same way. So, personalize networking to create an environment where both men and women can freely and happily network and take advantage of both business and career opportunities that arise. As Nicholas Cheffings, Senior Counsel and former Global Chair at Hogan Lovells, explained to me: 'make sure the male majority in leadership positions do not impose their norms on everyone else'.

If you have a budget for networking, make sure it isn't all funnelled into one or two big networking events in the year: spread it out, be inquisitive and find out how people want to network in your organization. When was the last time you asked?

While researching this book, I reached out to my LinkedIn network to gauge views on this topic. The responses indicated that some missed networking over the pandemic, some attended many more events online and didn't want to rush back to in-person evening events that eat into family time, some would like a mix of online and offline events and some would prefer coffee-time networking. Some may have previously expressed a preference for evening networking to 'keep up' and 'be present', but it could be that by asking your people what they need, it's not just those in the minority that want a different way of doing things.

A bit like the future world of offices, I see the hybrid model of networking working, a little magic online and a little magic in person.

Vanessa Vallely OBE, CEO and Founder of WeAreTheCity and WeAreTechWomen

So, before you design a strategy, ask what your employees want.

- What type of events would you prefer to attend?
- What time of day would you prefer events to take place?
- Would you prefer online or offline events, or a mixture of both?

Once you have asked your employees what they want, you can start to create a hybrid approach to networking so that individuals can align with the opportunities that suit them best. By mapping your employees' needs across several different types of events, you will have a better chance of finding a fruitful solution for all.

Jennie Koo, who is on the management board of Women in Banking and Finance, told me that variety is key to successful networking. She said: 'I'd like networking to be more readily and easily accessible to all, whether that be time, location, price or environment so that's where a mix of face-to-face, remote, virtual or purely digital would be a good start.'

Here is a menu of networking ideas to consider:

Online social media

For some, networking doesn't need to be face-to-face. You can build great relationships on platforms like LinkedIn and other social media communication channels. Encourage your people to actively and regularly use these platforms.

Virtual events

When the pandemic pushed all events into the virtual world, we experienced a new way of networking. I heard of a wheelchair user who said that during the pandemic, for the first time, she could attend virtual networking events and people saw her for who she was rather than seeing her chair before her. Virtual networking transformed her experience and enjoyment.

Many say that the best virtual events have either been attended by small numbers of people with a clear purpose, or where they have been able to connect easily with one other person in a break-out space. At one conference everyone had a button they could press at any time to get partnered up with a person at random, just like you might bump into someone in a queue for drinks.

Net-walking

Building supplies company, Wickes Group Plc, introduced a 'Walk and Talk' initiative, to recreate the missing watercooler moments you get in the office. Every two weeks, everyone within the 120-person digital and marketing team was given the opportunity to put their name into a random generator and was matched with another person – they then received an email telling them who they were paired with so that they could reach out and arrange a time to chat. The conversation had to be non-work-related, conducted by telephone, rather than a video chat, and they were encouraged to go out and walk to get exercise, too. In a hybrid-working world, this is a great way to create connections across organizations, especially for those that perhaps don't enjoy large events; it also supports wellbeing by encouraging people to get out and exercise while chatting. Wickes has said this has been a great way for them to continue to build and deepen relationships. Another organization runs 'coffee roulettes' where you go for a coffee with someone you're matched with (and the matching is done on things like 'what kind of coffee do you like?' or 'where is your dream holiday destination?').

In-person networking

Those who get energy from other people, like me, love face-to-face networking. However, the pandemic gave us permission to think about breaking the rule book and not necessarily go back to big networking events. Keep them small. Keep them informal. Keep them on purpose. Keep them gender neutral. Depending on the feedback from your people, consider running events like cooking demonstrations, wine tastings, wildlife walks, afternoon tea, book talks, private cinema screenings. A focus and purpose to an event helps people feel they can build their skills or knowledge and provides something to hang conversations on during mingling.

Be inclusive

Most importantly, be inclusive: if networking is important for everyone to build future relationships at work, be thoughtful and ask questions about what suits your people. To promote a sense of wellbeing, organizations could think about providing opportunities to network during the business day – perhaps at lunchtime or over coffee in the morning or afternoon. Many people – and not just women – want to take a break from work events in the evenings to spend time with friends and family, exercise, and do other things that are important to them. And most importantly make sure it is prioritized as a must-do, rather than a nice-to-do, so business as usual doesn't prevent attendance.

Offer training and resources to support with networking

As networking can be daunting, organizations can also offer their people the support to give them the best chance of success. This could include training around how to:

- **Create a 'people plan' or carry out a 'network audit'.** Vanessa Vallely OBE, one of the UK's most well-networked women, recommends that everyone creates a people plan at the start of the year. Encourage your people to think strategically about: Who do I need to meet? What do I need? Is there a potential mentor or sponsor within that group? Who can I help? This can be used as a framework to build connections throughout the year. And before you attend an event try to find out who is going so you can plan a purposeful connection.

- **Raise your profile and develop your personal brand.** Provide workshops or webinars to give your people time to consider what they need to do differently to amplify their impact, both internally and externally. Encourage them to actively take the time to use online social media platforms and attend networking events.

- **Develop networking skills.** Offer workshops that cover topics like the bridging technique, how to enter and exit conversations and the importance of listening skills – being interested first and interesting second.

Top tips on flexible networking

⊚ Ask your people how they want to network in your organization. It might surprise you!

⊚ Create a framework for a hybrid and inclusive model of networking, with both virtual and in-person opportunities and events. Ensure there is a focus and purpose to each event and find areas of joint interest that men and women can enjoy together.

⊚ Consider implementing a 'net-walking' initiative to create new connections and offer wellbeing support.

⊚ Provide opportunities to network during business hours to promote an inclusive culture and ensure that people, particularly women with childcare responsibilities, are not automatically excluded.

⊚ Monitor and track who attends your networking events to ensure inclusivity and help with planning future events and activities.

⊚ Encourage men to attend any women's events that they are invited to.

⊚ Offer your people training and resources to support networking.

⊚ Consider some alcohol-free events.

One of the most important things businesses need to do urgently is to reframe the narrative around gender equality: we need to move away from considering it to be a women's issue to be discussed, solved and fought for by women, when in reality, it affects everyone including men. Whether it is men's emotional wellbeing, their ability to spend more time with their children, or pursuing 'non-traditional' career paths such as nursing – equality for women is progress for all.

Simon Gallow, Advocate and HeForShe Lead,
UN Women UK

Chapter 3

Allyship

This chapter explores:

- ◎ how creating a culture of allyship can progress gender equality
- ◎ being aware of your own biases
- ◎ what type of ally you are and how you can create SPACES™ for women
- ◎ the importance of sponsorship
- ◎ how reverse mentoring plays a part in gender allyship.

Alongside flexibility, the second cultural framework that can progress gender equality within organizations is to create a culture of allyship where men are engaged as allies and not alienated from the gender debate. Men can be passionate advocates for gender equality – often inspired by the experiences of their female colleagues, wives, daughters, sisters and nieces – but often they don't know what to do, or understand what support they need to become a workplace ally. Indeed, research by Boston Consulting Group[47] found that in companies where men play a role in gender equality policies, 96% reported progress, compared with 30% where they do not.

> We know we cannot achieve our aims without engaging men as our allies. They are a critical piece of the puzzle.
>
> *Jacqueline Abbott-Deane, CEO, One Loud Voice for Women*

Here is one definition of allyship from the book *Good Guys* by David G. Smith and W. Brad Johnson: 'Actively promoting gender fairness and equity in the workplace through supportive and collaborative personal relationships and public acts of sponsorship and advocacy intended to drive systemic improvements to the workplace culture'.[48]

Even though the focus for this chapter is on male allies, women can play an equal part in being an ally to fellow women and others in a minority. Everyone stands to benefit from a culture of allyship.

Recognizing bias

Before we delve into how we can be better allies, let's explore why we need allies in the first place. One of the reasons why women are still not reaching more senior positions is because of unconscious or implicit bias. Unconscious biases are inherent in all of us and are social stereotypes that we form about certain groups of people affecting our decisions and how we communicate with people every day. Affinity bias, or similarity bias, occurs when we treat people more favourably, simply because they are like us. When it comes to promotions, leaders (and we know the majority are men) tend to seek out people who look and sound like them, are interested in the same things, and who are in the same networks.

Recognizing and avoiding affinity bias at work is key to creating diverse teams. Many organizations now implement blind recruitment processes and offer unconscious bias training to staff. However, it has been questioned whether unconscious bias training works. The Government Equalities Office[49] scrapped its scheme, stating there was 'no evidence' that the training improved workplace equality.

What is clear is that organizations need to stop using unconscious bias and diversity training as a quick fix (or even worse, as a box-ticking exercise). What is needed is greater cultural change, and this is where creating an allies culture can really make big change happen.

This section of the book explores what an ally is, why it is so important to engage men in the debate, where you sit on the Gender Allies Matrix™ and steps men can take to become better allies in the workplace, including the benefits of sponsorship and reverse mentoring.

Being an ally takes courage. Great allies sponsor others and use their voice and influence on behalf of someone else. They call out what others do, whether this is positive or negative, and are not afraid to be curious about their own attitudes and assumptions. An ally recognizes that, while they are not a member of the marginalized group they support, they should make a concerted effort to better understand the obstacles which individuals from that marginalized group face. The majority must drive the change.

The Gender Allies Matrix™

The Gender Allies Matrix™ that I developed looks at how you can show up as an ally. The vertical axis looks at the actions you take, and the horizontal axis looks at your personal beliefs around gender equality. It is unusual for someone to be in one box only and typically people display all four characteristics at different times and in different circumstances. So, you're unlikely to be a 100% Champion, although you may be! Depending on how much you believe in gender equality and the actions you are taking, there are four different ally types that are identified:

- **Ostriches** don't see why they need to change the status quo. They are quite happy with the way things have always been done and are apathetic to change. They may not even believe gender inequality exists – a view held by one in seven (15%) Britons.[50] They are also potentially fearful that their jobs are going to be lost to women. They put their heads in the sand and don't engage in conversations on this subject.

- **Performers**, also known as performative allies, show off support visibly when there is a direct gain for them and when it suits them. This might be to help progress into a new role, to put on their CV or for a 'pat on the back' on social media. They may be more inclined to 'say' rather than 'do'.

- **Apprentices** are eager to learn how to be a better ally. They believe and know there is still a lot that needs to be done to move the dial. They may have colleagues, daughters, wives, sisters or nieces they are keen to support, but don't know where to start. They are eager to learn but need direction and support from others to give them the courage to start and know what action they need to take.

- **Champions** believe strongly in supporting women and those in a minority, and they are not afraid to act on their convictions and encourage others to do the same. They go over and above to show their support and are happy to be a lone voice around the table when discussing and supporting these issues.

Have a look at the matrix and think about how you currently show up at work in relation to being an ally to women in your organization. Think about what proportion of your time and focus is spent showing up as the different types outlined. Once you have done this, and depending where you spend most of your time, look at the steps in the 'Where to start?' section below and take some practical next steps using the SPACES™ framework (on page 63).

Figure 2: The Gender Allies Matrix™

How do you currently show up at work in relation to gender equality?
Rate each box as a % of your time and focus

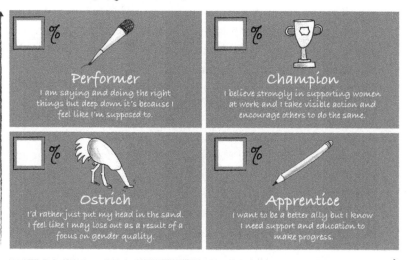

Where to start?

It is the role of leaders and those in a majority to fix the problem of inequality. The same goes for any equality campaign. Take Black Lives Matter. It is up to the majority to fix the problem, not the black community. A good starting point is to ask questions that show interest and don't be afraid to say the wrong thing. Show your vulnerability and admit it if you're not sure how to offer support.

Another step is addressing harassment, which is still being reported all too frequently in the workplace. A study by Deloitte shows that a majority of women (59%) have experienced harassment and/or microaggressions over the past year at work. Ninety-three per cent of women believe their employer will not take action if they report non-inclusive behaviours and 93% of women believe reporting non-inclusive behaviours will impact their careers.[51]

We all need to be very aware of language and speak up if we hear or see anything inappropriate. I was once told by a partner in a consulting firm that I would need to 'sleep my way to the top'. I hope that these types of comments are much less frequent today, but we need to work hard to eradicate them completely.

Julia Muir, author of the book *Change the Game*, explains that male leaders are important role models to other men, so need to set a good example and recognize both inclusive behaviour and incivility: 'Men need to ensure microaggressions are called out and hostile workplace cultures are not tolerated. We're still at a point where men will take more notice if other men are calling it out than if women are, particularly if the men are more senior'.[52]

Richard Pickard, CEO of Inclusive Search, says that to be a great ally your words and actions must be in sync and he suggests six ways to do this:

- lift others up by advocating
- share growth opportunities with others

- recognize inequality and systems which foster it
- realize the impact of microaggressions
- appreciate under-represented people's lived experiences
- listen, self-reflect and change.

If you are at the start of this journey, take some time to:

Educate yourself

- Read books (see Further reading and resources section on page 217), attend gender employee networks, attend training courses on being an ally and explore your own biases and how these show up for you.
- Start having conversations with female colleagues – be curious, listen and learn.

Recognize your own privilege

- Men, white people, heterosexual people, able-bodied people and those from comfortable socio-economic backgrounds all have privilege: contrast this with anyone who is in a minority. There is a powerful graphic called the Wheel of Privilege in an Everywoman report called 'Inclusion into Action' that illustrates privilege beautifully.[53]
- Understand how fortunate you are and how others around you have not necessarily had this privilege. Take time to think about how the world perceives and, therefore, benefits you. Acknowledging your own privilege helps you become more aware of the disadvantages faced by those in a minority and sets the tone for more inclusive behaviours. As sociologist Professor Michael Kimmel said: 'Privilege is invisible to those who have it.'[54]
- Can you remember a time in your life where you have felt excluded? How did it feel?

> We all have privilege – it's about how we use it and spend it to create opportunities for others which is important.
>
> *Belinda Riley, Diversity, Equity and Inclusion Consultant*

Show up and be visible

- Talk to your colleagues (regardless of their gender or ethnicity) about what you learnt at events or on training courses relating to diversity.
- Be curious and ask more questions.
- Share more widely why you have chosen to commit to becoming an ally.
- Write internally about why equality and inclusion matters to you and what you are doing.
- Don't be a bystander: call out inappropriate language, banter and microaggressions.

Create SPACES™ for women

The following SPACES™ framework was designed for the allies workshops I run for organizations. It was developed to inspire action and commitment to becoming an ally for women and is designed so that organizations, or aspiring allies who feel overwhelmed and are not sure where to begin, can start small, pick one of the tasks and get going.

These are the SPACES™ actions the framework covers:

- Sponsor
- Pass on opportunities
- Act with insight
- Communicate with curiosity
- Engage women in meetings
- Set an example.

Figure 3: The SPACES™ framework

Sponsor

Actively champion and promote women to other people

Why?

Sponsorship is known to be one of the most influential things for any individual's career progression, and even more important for women who have fewer 'informal' sponsorship arrangements in place.

How?

Think of one woman you would willingly sponsor for promotion, a project or greater visibility. Find 36 minutes in your diary this week: Take her out for a 30-minute coffee, spend five minutes congratulating her on a success in a meeting and find one minute to recommend her to someone else.

Pass on opportunities

Look in your diary and see what you don't need to be involved in

Why?

Women aren't offered as many opportunities as men typically because of affinity bias (where we gravitate towards people like ourselves in appearance and beliefs).

How?

In the next month, find a meeting or opportunity you can pass to a female colleague. How will you ask them if they would like this opportunity?

Act with insight

Think about other people's personal circumstances before your own

Why?

Women will continue to miss out on opportunities if individual circumstances are not taken into account.

How?

Create a culture and process for 'non-negotiables' – what one thing per week do each of your team members want to put in their diary? Yoga class, dog walk, child pick-up, etc.

Audit your team get-togethers – where and when do they take place? Do they suit everyone?

Communicate with curiosity
Don't make assumptions and be brave to ask questions about how you can support

Why?

If you don't ask, you won't learn and the same patterns of behaviour will continue.

How?

Have regular check-ins with your female colleagues and listen to what it's like to be a woman in your organization. Take action to support them. When you see someone expressing sexist language, call them out: 'see something, say something'.

Engage women in meetings
Provide structure and facilitation for balanced airtime in meetings

Why?

Some people get overshadowed by those who speak the loudest (admittedly this could be a woman too!) and if their voices are not heard, the quieter voices will not get their points across. In time, this will make them invisible when it comes to promotions.

How?

Structure meetings so that everyone gets time to express their views before a free-flowing discussion.

When a woman speaks, build on and amplify what she says and avoid interruptions. If you know someone is usually quiet, chat to them in advance and ask if there is anything you can do to support them in the meeting.

Set an example
Role-model what you want to see and remember that people will follow what you do, not what you say

Why?

If you don't, the unwritten rule will be to follow your example. If you don't talk about picking your kids up from school, or going outside for a walk to get a screen break, no one else will feel comfortable doing so.

How?

Publicly leave the office for family or exercise, etc. Acknowledge mistakes and make collaboration a priority.

Make sure that you're not seen to join in with dodgy jokes or banter. Challenge systems and processes that may be unintentionally biased.

Top tips on allyship

- Use the Gender Allies Matrix™ framework within your organization. Encourage all colleagues to establish where they sit on the grid, and provide guidance on how they can step up and spend more time as Champions. Explain the 'why' – what change are you expecting to see as a result?

- Provide training on how to be a better workplace ally and create SPACES™ for women.

- Encourage those in senior positions to role-model inclusive behaviours and actions that support women from the top.

- Don't be afraid to make mistakes.

- Recognize that new habits take time to form, and old habits can create big barriers to change. Encourage people to work together so they can say something and speak up if old behaviours start sneaking in (e.g., if someone is always speaking over others in meetings).

- Be mindful of performative allyship, i.e., just doing something because you think it's the right thing to do. This can undermine the whole purpose of allyship and can disengage women.

- Build allies objectives into performance evaluations. Management guru Peter Drucker is credited with the much-used phrase, 'What gets measured gets managed'.[55] Celebrate and reward men and women who actively champion, support and promote women – this will have a cascading effect.

The first 'S' of the SPACES™ framework is 'Sponsor' – to actively champion and promote women to other people. The following section examines what sponsorship is, and how this simple act can remove some of the obstacles faced by women on the path to leadership.

Clearing the path through sponsorship

Three quarters of senior leaders agree that sponsorship supports the promotion of talent, yet only 3% of female leaders are sponsored.[56] This means a whopping 97% are not!

> Sponsorship is one of the most critical things to career success that we often forget about… having a really good sponsor, that person who is your advocate throughout the organization makes all the difference.
>
> *Sian Prigg, Senior Learning and Talent Manager, Opel Vauxhall Finance and Founder of Start Sooner*[57]

In 2019 my own research found that 51% of respondents wanted their organization to offer internal sponsorship, compared to 25% of respondents who said their organization currently offered it.[58]

A formal system for sponsorship has the capability to cut through established patterns of systemic and unconscious gender bias and increase the visibility and impact of female employees. It also unlocks myriad other benefits for women, including networking, allyship and mentoring. However, despite the clear benefits of sponsorship, only a fifth of senior leaders report formal sponsorship programmes in the organizations they work with.[59]

If every organization prioritizes sponsorship, the speed at which women reach more senior roles will accelerate.

> Sponsorship helps us to navigate around an organization and can open up opportunities to women that allow them to develop and succeed.
>
> *Virginia Simmons, Managing Partner UK & Ireland, McKinsey & Company*

What is a sponsor?

A sponsor is someone senior in an organization that uses their social and political capital for others. In the context of this book, this would be for a woman they know and respect. They become an ally to this woman and actively support her by knowing about the work and value she brings and will take steps to help her get over any obstacles she might face on the path to leadership. They might introduce her to influential connections, highlight her work to senior leaders, or recommend her for jobs and promotions. They are an advocate in the room. A mentor, on the other hand, offers advice and guidance to help navigate a career path. A sponsor can also be a mentor, but a mentor is not automatically a sponsor.

Why is sponsorship so important for women?

Women tend to believe that their work will speak for itself, but in reality those that shout the loudest, or have someone shouting for them, are the ones that will get a seat at the top table. Sadly, meritocracy doesn't exist in the workplace; it is not enough to just get your head down and work hard. You may be lucky, but it's unlikely a promotion or step up the ladder will magically appear. Sponsors can ensure women get experience in the best career-defining roles, working on the right projects so that once it gets to performance review stage, you are not saying things like 'this woman hasn't had the relevant experience due to her time out of the business to be considered alongside this other person'.

Julie Baker is Head of Enterprise, Climate Engagement and Partnerships at NatWest Group. She attributes some of her success to a line manager she had when she was appointed in her first leadership position 30 years ago: 'I had a wonderful line manager at the time, he took me to one side, he really supported me. And he really made me step out of my comfort zone to build up that confidence. If he hadn't done that and given me the confidence and the skills to look after commercial clients, I wouldn't be doing what I'm doing today. I do owe him a lot.' As she said to me, managers need to recognize that career progression is different for women, and they need sponsors and support. Accept that women may need a nudge to put themselves forward and achieve their full potential.

Beware of unconscious and affinity bias

Of course, sponsorship is important for men too. However, they are more likely to receive sponsorship than women, given that unconscious and affinity bias means male leaders tend to sponsor and support those who are like them. These informal sponsorship relationships can potentially impede rather than boost diversity, creating a cycle in which men sponsor other men; in fact, this type of informal sponsorship can do more harm than good.

It is important that organizations create *formal*, as opposed to informal, sponsorship programmes, to allow everyone the chance to be visible at the promotion conversation. And this sponsorship needs to be active, visible and accountable.

Case Study: Sponsorship at Reed Smith LLP

Reed Smith LLP, an international law firm, runs a Women's Initiative called WINRS. This has transformed how women are supported, evaluated and promoted through a combination of focused programmes, sponsorship and other initiatives.

One initiative is its Mastermind Programme, which is designed to position its women lawyers (specifically senior associates and counsel) for promotion. Each year, approximately 30 high-potential women are identified to participate in the programme, which links each one of the eligible woman lawyers with a strategic sponsor in the firm. The sponsor provides mentoring and sponsorship, as needed, to advocate and strategize with the lawyer regarding her advancement.

The programme is designed to ensure that female lawyers on the path to promotion have the skills they need to advance to the next level. It covers topics including oral advocacy skills, understanding the business aspect of the firm and the metrics that make up the business case for promotion, time management, leadership development and building a professional network. Sponsors also provide advice on what it takes to develop and own a practice, how to create and develop an effective business plan and how to build and develop strong networks within and outside the firm.

However, most importantly, the programme focuses on a strategic alignment with a sponsor, who will work with the lawyer to ensure that she is well-positioned for advancement and advocate for her at promotion time.

The success of the programme is clear. It is measured by looking at promotion successes and attrition data, with many beneficiaries of the programme being promoted as a result. One woman who has benefitted is Laura Riddeck: 'The sponsorship initiative was very helpful in clarifying my thoughts and approach to promotion. It was particularly useful to discuss strategies with someone from outside my department, who was able to offer a different perspective.'

Top tips on sponsorship

- Implement a formal sponsorship programme that includes awareness and understanding of the obstacles that women face. They should be in every organization by default and as common as conducting annual appraisals.
- If you do nothing else after reading this book, sponsor a woman! Even better, encourage other colleagues to do the same. And even better, implement a sponsorship programme in your organization.
- 'Sponsor' the sponsor programme – as with any new initiative, ensure the programme is led from the top down.
- Define clearly what sponsorship is and the objectives of the programme, so it doesn't get confused with mentoring or other career development initiatives.
- Provide training to sponsors to ensure they understand what is expected of them and keep them accountable by building sponsorship objectives into performance evaluations.
- Set up key performance indicators up front, so you can track the success of the programme.
- Avoid unconscious bias and preferential treatment by ensuring a formal matching process is in place. Don't leave it to sponsors to identify their own 'sponsees'.

The role of reverse mentoring

Alongside sponsorship, another allyship initiative for improving the chances of women reaching leadership positions is mentoring. Mentoring programmes have been shown to boost minority representation at management level by 9% to 24%, and dramatically improve promotion and retention rates for minorities and women from 15% to 38%.[60] And, of course, mentoring programmes are not just something for women. All employees can clearly benefit. However, this book is looking at ways to progress women and so this is the focus here.

There are several ways that mentoring can be structured, but I want to shine a light on reverse mentoring as a way of progressing gender equality. This can provide an understanding of the lived experiences of people who are different to you as well as closing the perception gap that exists between how leaders and others experience the culture of the organization. Whether or not you have a reverse mentoring programme in place, and whatever the objectives of that programme, this section will help you understand the role of reverse mentoring, the benefits for the mentor, mentee and the organization, and top tips for implementing a successful reverse mentoring programme.

What is reverse mentoring?

Reverse mentoring has traditionally been used to help retain millennial talent, help senior executives become more sophisticated about social media and other digital skills, drive culture change and understand younger clients and customers. However, it can also be used to progress gender equality in the workplace, as it helps senior men understand and learn from female employees' experiences. It works by pairing junior female employees with a senior executive (either male or female) to exchange insights, reflections and feedback on a variety of topics. This can include technology, collaboration, productivity, different ways of working and communication. This is the opposite of traditional mentoring – where a senior, more experienced person advises a junior employee.

According to a McKinsey & Company study, *Women in the Workplace 2020*: 'For the sixth year in a row, women continued to lose ground at the first step up to manager. For every 100 men promoted to manager, only 85 women were promoted.'[61] Pairing a high-potential, mid-career woman with a more senior decision-maker (either male or female) can bring about enormous benefits for both the mentee and mentor, as well as foster inclusion and diversity for the organization. The best way to grow, evolve and achieve gender balance in the workplace is to learn from people who are *not* like you.

> Reverse mentoring has worked brilliantly at Wickes and has enabled us to support younger women in the organization to have a voice. It is definitely a two-way street and has brought benefits to both parties. It has also given our leaders a greater degree of empathy with individuals and rational compassion for the women at Wickes.
>
> *Gary Kibble, Chief Marketing Officer, Wickes Group Plc*

Case study: The benefits of reverse mentoring

I interviewed a reverse mentoring pair from the Royal Bank of Canada (RBC) to help me understand the benefits. RBC's 'Diversity Dialogues' programme matches individuals to someone with a completely different background to themselves. Meerah Azhar, who was formerly an associate director at RBC, was mentor to the Chief Operating Officer, David Bailey. They found their reverse mentoring incredibly valuable. Here's what I learnt.

Benefits for the junior female mentor

Meerah Azhar explained: 'Having the ability to interact with a leader who is not your direct manager is so useful. I share insights and learning on how business strategy is playing out on the ground, and what is and isn't working. This is incredibly valuable and makes me feel empowered and passionate about what I'm doing and where I work. I have been very lucky to have someone who shares freely and honestly. I can ask him questions and he is always very open and honest with his answers. This allowed me to find courage to challenge and gain confidence.'

Frequent feedback, recognition and encouragement from someone more senior can boost confidence and help women to progress into more senior positions that they may not have believed they were capable of. Women tend to evaluate their performance less favourably than men and can often feel undervalued and unappreciated.

Having access to someone more senior in the organization can help women to navigate their career with more success by:

- **Providing exposure to senior leadership** and being involved in strategic and organizational thinking. This gives junior female employees the opportunity to gain insight into a leader's mindset and witness what they are trying to achieve. As they grow within the company, they know what is important and can frame their thinking to align with considerations for the future. They also get to see how teams are led before moving into people management.

- **Feeling empowered to share thoughts and insights** on organizational strategy, how it is playing out on the ground, and what is and isn't working. This helps prepare the foundations for stepping into leadership positions in the future.

- **Being a safe space to build confidence** in presenting to a senior person. Being a reverse mentor can be nerve-wracking in the first instance, as the mentee is more senior and is often perceived as being highly successful. However, reverse mentoring provides a safe space for more junior employees to find courage to challenge and gain confidence interacting with senior people.

- **Facilitating introductions to new networks.** The access to someone more senior can facilitate introductions to new networks so that the mentor can increase their visibility, which is important for future career opportunities.

- **Providing a forum for being heard.** It creates an opportunity to raise personal concerns and those of other female colleagues, ask for career advice and be more aware of potential opportunities. If the relationship is good, reverse mentoring can also be a natural route to sponsorship, and the mentee will be more likely to represent them when it comes to promotion conversations.

Benefits for the senior male mentee

David Bailey (Chief Operating Officer, RBC Wealth Management) said: 'I would highly recommend reverse mentoring to my peers, but I would stress not doing it for box-ticking purposes. Go into it because you want to learn from it and get better at what you do. I try to support and help my mentors as much as they help me. For example, one of my mentors asked for my advice on how to deal with a manager who is a bottleneck for decision-making. As well as being able to offer advice to her, it also made me reflect and consider whether I am ever like this. I try not to be, but I know I can be a bit of a control freak! So, I went away to check that I'm not removing the accountability from people who should be making those decisions.'

Taking part in a mentoring programme, of any kind, can sometimes feel like a drain on a leader's already precious time, but those that do participate find that the benefits very much outweigh the time commitment. A mentee in a reverse mentoring relationship can benefit from:

- **Having someone more junior help justify the decisions they make,** the way they think about things and what is driving them to make certain decisions. It helps them to get a different perspective and understand how certain decisions play out with different demographics in the business.

- **Gaining different perspectives** and an understanding of the gender and diversity challenges women face within the organization. This gives the mentee an opportunity to learn what changes can be made to create an environment that works better for women.

Benefits for the organization

In addition to the benefits for both mentee and mentor, the organizational benefits of reverse mentoring are plenty:

- **Increased visibility of mid-career women** in the organization. Reverse mentoring gives women an opportunity to be seen and heard by senior decision-makers, which, in turn, can help inform promotion and pay decisions for high potential employees.

- **Promotes an understanding of the gender and diversity challenges women face** within the organization and what changes can be made to create an environment that works for women including changes to pay, parental policies and ways of working.

- **Creates a more inclusive culture of listening and learning.** This becomes a cascading benefit as the mentors can become the mentees in time, and will have worked in an environment that is inclusive and open to listening to different viewpoints.

- **Enables a network of different relationships** and connections across the organization that otherwise would not be made.

- **Supports personal development plans** in creating more confident and competent female employees, as well as pushing senior individuals out of their comfort zone by engaging with what can sometimes be uncomfortable topics.

@ **Shifts 'assumed' power away from the senior ranks** – helping those that are in the majority understand their privilege and unconscious biases.

@ **Shows employees that they are providing a safe space for conversations** between female staff and more senior colleagues.

Another organization that is very well versed in reverse mentoring is professional services firm PwC. It launched its first reverse mentoring programme in 2014 as part of its diversity and inclusion drive. The programme had at least 120 millennials mentoring 200 partners and directors, with the mentors meeting once a month with their mentees. PwC has changed its focus recently to incorporate ethnic diversity, fuelled by the Black Lives Matter campaign, and it currently has a programme involving 50 partners.

Like the gender conversation, our predominantly white and male partner group (of which I am one), don't always know how to talk about ethnic diversity and some of us were scared we would say the wrong thing. We are constantly asking our people what we should be focusing on and it's important to us that any reverse mentoring programme supports the current needs of our people and partners.

Antony Cook, Partner, PwC

Another professional services firm, Deloitte, ran a powerful reverse mentoring programme where 'almost half of the participants were promoted since the pilot began'.[62]

Top tips on reverse mentoring

- If you haven't yet got a reverse mentoring programme in place, be careful not to just hand it over to your HR team to implement. This type of initiative needs to be led from the top of the organization and visibly promoted as a strategic tool in supporting employees. Make it personal and don't allow it to become a box-ticking exercise.

- Step back and consider the business benefits of putting a reverse mentoring programme in place to support gender equality: What will change as a result? How will the programme link to your business objectives?

- Match women who might feel they are facing obstacles at work with senior decision-makers, either male or female. Consider how you will get as many women to benefit as possible and cascade it down the organization.

- Mix individuals across departments, locations and different areas of the business, and don't put two similar personality types together (e.g., two introverts). Online matching software is available, which can help match individuals rather than completing the process manually.

- Keep it virtual to provide opportunities for mixing across locations and a neutral safe space in which to discuss ideas.

- Consult mentees (the more senior individual) before formalizing pairing, to check for any conflicts of interest.

- Consider the structure of the programme. A schedule of one-hour sessions each month for six to nine months seems to work well. Switch mentors regularly to avoid relationships going stale and keep in touch as things move on.

◉ Ensure there is a strong commitment from both parties and sessions are not cancelled – this is often the biggest reason why mentoring doesn't work.

◉ Offer flexible guidelines on topics relating to gender, culture and career progression as a starting point for discussion but avoid formulaic rules and leave this to the pairing to decide. The mentor (i.e., the female) should lead the meeting: it works well to have a framework, but not so structured that it stifles the flow of ideas and creativity or stops any freedom to go off topic or in a different direction.

◉ Have a training programme and check-ins for mentors to learn from each other. Research shows that without training, only one third of mentor–mentee relationships succeed. [63]

◉ Consider how you will measure the impact of the programme to establish whether it has been successful. This could be feedback via surveys or email, individual or group discussions, observing a change in behaviour in meetings, and tracking progression and retention of participants.

The next chapter looks at the third and final cultural framework, which is how coaching and support can help to create more gender-balanced businesses.

Organizations wishing to maximize the benefits of coaching should focus on increasing its scope and availability to create a coaching culture that permeates throughout their workforce.

Institute of Leadership and Management[64]

Chapter 4

Coaching and support

This chapter explores:

- ◎ how a culture of coaching supports a gender-balanced business
- ◎ different types of coaching interventions
- ◎ the benefits of coaching
- ◎ how to create a culture of coaching in your organization.

Creating a coaching culture within your organization will maximize the potential of each and every one of your people and will provide a solid foundation for a more gender-balanced workplace.

There are different ways in which you can bring coaching into the fabric of your organization; this could be using professional external or internal coaches, running group coaching programmes, offering peer-to-peer coaching, or 'growing your own' coaches, where every manager is trained in key coaching skills. Coaching for gender equality can include supporting women with the obstacles they face (see Part 3) as well as supporting others in becoming better allies and more confident inclusive leaders.

Sadly, coaching is often put in the 'too expensive' box, or is reserved for senior leadership teams (which we know can be predominantly male). Research in the US of 18,000 employees shows that there is a coaching gender divide and more men are given access to coaching than women (22% compared to 16%).[65] Be mindful of who is offered coaching and ensure that men and women benefit equally.

Coaching can bring many benefits for career progression. Here is some feedback from a selection of participants on our coaching programmes: 'It has given me renewed focus and direction on being a better leader', 'I was pushed out of my comfort zone but that was exactly what I needed', 'My coach helped me to open up new possibilities that I thought weren't possible', 'I feel more equipped to lead my team in a constructive and efficient way' and 'I've taken the lead on a number of projects with much more confidence'.

> True gender equality comes from developing each employee regardless of gender.
>
> *Christopher Fairbank, The Dare to be Different Business Leadership Strategist*[66]

How to create a culture of coaching and support

By adopting a coaching mindset and cascading coaching practices across your organization, coaching will become an integral part of everything you do and will support a gender-balanced business.

Alison Hardingham describes a coaching culture as: 'A culture where people coach each other all the time as a natural part of meetings, reviews and one-to-one discussions of all kinds.'[67] Only 13% of companies surveyed by the International Coaching Federation[68] reported that they have achieved an organization-wide coaching culture. Are you a leader who is helping your people to grow and thrive by having conversations and expressing interest, listening actively and offering honest feedback? If your organization operates more within a learning culture (e.g., training and telling), as opposed to a coaching culture (i.e., listening and asking), think about ways in which you can shift the balance, starting with your team and letting this ripple out more widely.

Bring in more regular check-ins and feedback, instead of reserving these conversations for annual performance reviews; in the sporting world, a coach wouldn't wait a whole year before providing feedback to an athlete following a race. The same applies in business. Immediate feedback, through regular check-ins, is much more valuable, especially when people are working remotely. Research has also found that men receive more actionable feedback than women at work.[69]

> We have an everyday coaching model which we use and that's really trying to encourage employees and line managers to coach in every situation that's available.
>
> *Rhonda Howarth, formerly Head of Learning & Development and Global HR Transformation Lead at Nestlé*[70]

Decide on your portfolio of coaching interventions

Once you are ready to put coaching into practice, you can decide what your coaching strategy should be, and which combination of coaching interventions will work best for you: this decision can be based on resources available, the number of people at each level of your organization you'd like to offer coaching to and individuals' needs. For example, you may decide that you want to focus on giving your managers training in how to have great coaching conversations (perhaps bringing in external support for this training), or you may want to recruit and develop some internal coaches. Whatever combination you prefer, try to ensure that there is a fair and equitable process in place for selecting who benefits from all levels in the organization and that it is not merely a benefit for the top tier of leadership.

Different coaching interventions that can be used in any combination in your organization include:

- 1-2-1 coaching (using an external provider or an internal coach)
- Group coaching (facilitated by internal or external coach)
- Coaching by line manager
- Peer-to-peer coaching.

There is a free download at www.dontfixwomen.com listing the pros and cons of these different types of coaching interventions.

Ensure internal coaches and managers are appropriately trained

Whatever type of coaching intervention you decide to use, if it includes using internal coaches and managers, make sure that you have the appropriate training in place to support them. A third of organizations do not offer any support or development for internal coaches, which can potentially do more harm than good.[71] Coaching skills can be a beneficial add-on to induction training, so that everyone joining the organization can learn how to have great coaching conversations.

Create a clear structure and process for coaching

Once you have decided what sort of coaching interventions you need (be open to this changing, depending on circumstances and needs), create a clear structure that can be communicated across your employee base, so that everyone knows what is available and to whom. Consider the coaching tools your coaches might employ – for example I developed a Wheel of Potential™ coaching framework that we use in our coaching programmes.

How can coaching specifically help women?

Coaching can help both men and women in different ways. Here I outline some of the ways that coaching can help women specifically. This is not about fixing women. This is about really understanding what individual challenges they face and what is holding them back in their career. This could be anything from returning from maternity leave, going through menopause, facing a job transition, to having the confidence to speak up with authenticity or suffering from imposter syndrome. Offering appropriate support and coaching to women as they face these obstacles is a small price to pay to reduce the cost of attrition and help more women progress to senior roles.

How coaching can be used to address gender imbalance

Coaching can bring a number of benefits for organizations in support of gender equality:

- Increased retention of women, saving money on recruitment costs (which can equate to around 6-9 months of salary).[72]

◎ Improved individual employee performance, leading to increased productivity and a better return on your investment for the women you have employed. Research shows a return on investment for companies of 10 to 49 times the investment made in coaching.[73]

◎ Women gain more confidence to face new challenges, step up in their current role and progress in their careers.

◎ Being able to demonstrate support and commitment to career development for your people, as well as support around health and wellbeing, especially for those who are working remotely.

◎ Individuals that have been coached are more likely to coach others, and cascade this into a coaching culture for your organization.

GSK (a large multinational pharmaceutical organization) carried out research in 2013, which assessed how coaching can be used to address gender imbalance at middle and senior leadership levels.[74] The *Accelerating Difference* initiative included 18 female leaders – each leader received a maximum of 12 individual coaching sessions, as well as six group coaching sessions, which were spread over 14 months (between five and seven female leaders were assigned to each group). Each session was approximately four hours in length.

The research concluded that coaching supported the development of female leaders in many ways, including enabling the development of skills and capabilities and boosting self-esteem, which led to increased self-belief and confidence to apply for and gain high-quality jobs and progression within the organization. This increased sense of self also allowed them to let go of the need to be known as a female leader and instead be viewed as a leader.

An additional benefit of the programme was that many women chose to give back by becoming coaches themselves, which created a ripple effect through the organization. In testament to this, the *Accelerating Difference* programme is still running and provides coaching to high-performing female managers. Over 1,100 women from 45 countries have benefitted from the *Accelerating Difference* programme since its launch. GSK's gender pay gap for all permanent UK based staff was 11.18% at the end of 2021, outperforming the national average of 14.9%.[75]

Case study: Turning confidence on its head through coaching

The following case study explains how coaching gave Helen Buttery, Lead HR Business Partner at Wickes Group Plc, a renewed confidence in her role to step out of her comfort zone and achieve things she hadn't felt were possible before.

She took part in a programme of 12 coaching sessions with one of my coaches, Kathryn Wakefield.

How did your coaching come about?

I was offered coaching during a review meeting with my line manager as a way for me to develop my confidence. Having not had coaching before, I wouldn't have even thought about coaching as a potential tool for overcoming my confidence challenges and this coaching intervention turned things around for me.

What kind of topics and challenges did you find it most useful to discuss?

My confidence was at an all-time low, and I was suffering from imposter syndrome. Kathryn took me on a journey that I wasn't expecting – delving into past jobs and experiences to get to the root cause of where my lack of confidence came from. I had been confident in the past, but in my previous job had suffered from a lot of stress as a result of one boss. I was so stressed and anxious about going to work, my hair started to fall out. I chose to walk away without a job. My coaching, using a variety of tools and frameworks, helped me to see where my current triggers were by spending time talking about my past experiences.

What tools did coaching provide you with?

Coaching helped me to recognize signs in my body and relieve moments of stress and anxiety through tools like breathing techniques. I was holding myself back in certain situations because I was worried about what might happen. The coaching gave me a gentle nudge to give it a try and challenged me to think 'what is the worst that could happen?' Having these new tools and resources at my fingertips when I recognize the signs has been phenomenal. One of the biggest things for me has been journaling and writing everything down. At night-time, emptying my head onto paper and stepping away. Something so simple, yet incredibly powerful.

What has the coaching helped you achieve?

The coaching has given me the confidence to step outside my comfort zone and raise my profile with stakeholders in the business. I stepped up to lead a new project which concluded in presenting a proposal to a board meeting for approval of an investment of just under £1m. This is not something I would have done before my coaching! The coaching gave me the confidence to liaise with my divisional director, which in turn give her confidence in my abilities. I got some great feedback from the HR director who said the difference compared to a presentation I did the previous year was unrecognizable. I now feel braver about setting clear boundaries and saying, for example, that I can't do an important presentation on the day my kids have gone back to school, as I know that I won't be in the best place to deliver this. It's important to recognize the external factors in your life and be confident to communicate this to others in your team.

How do you feel about the future now that you've had your coaching?

I feel excited! Looking back to when we started the coaching sessions, I couldn't even talk about career progression. My wellbeing and mental health have also improved and I feel empowered and I have a clear defined path that I'd like to take and I feel so much more confident.

Why is it important to have coaching?

The coaching allowed me to feel I deserve that place at the table. I now have the confidence to step into who I am irrespective of others' opinions of me. I'm always going to be a woman but I'm just as good as my male counterparts, and I love having a renewed sense of confidence and empowerment.

By creating a culture of coaching and support, employees will feel safe and empowered to express their ideas, make decisions freely, be open about their concerns, and actions can be taken to support everyone. Below are some top tips to help you navigate your way to a more coaching-based culture.

Top tips on coaching and support

- ◎ Establish if there is a budget for coaching and who is responsible for allocation.
- ◎ Regularly assess when a coaching intervention could be helpful (i.e., role transition, preparing for a promotion, dealing with some of the obstacles outlined in Part 3).
- ◎ Consider all types of coaching interventions and choose the most appropriate type of coaching for each situation that arises, e.g., would a peer-to-peer coaching programme be beneficial or do you need external help?
- ◎ Think about how you will measure return on investment. This could include tangible benefits (e.g., speaking up more), intangible benefits (e.g., communication style) and organizational benefits (e.g., impact on sales).
- ◎ Offer coaching at all levels of the organization, particularly where individuals are facing any of the obstacles that are covered in Part 3.
- ◎ Focus on actionable and effective feedback for your team – introduce regular check-ins as well as giving feedback in annual performance reviews.
- ◎ Ensure any internal coaches and managers are appropriately trained.
- ◎ Think about your own coaching skills and if you need help to develop these.
- ◎ Create a structure and process for coaching and communicate this clearly.

What next?

We have now looked at how to prepare the ground for gender equality by creating three cultural frameworks to make big change happen: flexibility, allyship, and coaching and support.

Alongside developing these three cultural frameworks to progress gender equality, organizations can focus on removing the obstacles that women face on their path to leadership. In Part 3, I have distilled the challenges that I know many women can face into three main areas of focus:

- Hormonal challenges (also referred to as the four Ms): menopause, maternity, miscarriage and fertility issues, and monthlies.
- Caring responsibilities: childcare, eldercare, and wellbeing and self-care.
- Confidence at work.

At the end of each chapter, I provide workplace solutions categorized by the cultural frameworks I have outlined in this part. By taking on board the suggestions in the book, you will start to make a difference. And the by-product of making these changes? It will create a more supportive and happier workplace for everyone.

It makes total sense that happiness is linked to a positive working environment and a positive working environment tends to correlate with being treated fairly. If you have equality, you have autonomy and opportunity.

James Bailey, Executive Director, Waitrose (John Lewis Partnership)

Part 3

Understanding the obstacles that women face at work

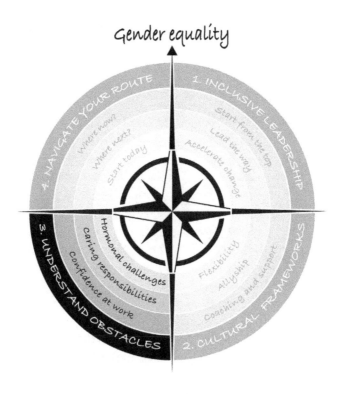

One in three women considered downshifting their career or leaving the workforce in 2021[76]: the question we should ask ourselves is, why?

For decades, women have talked about juggling their careers with family and home life. Denise Wilson OBE, in her Foreword, likens the load that women carry to rocks in a rucksack, slowing down progression on their career path.

To make the shift towards more equal career progression for men and women, companies need to help clear the obstacles that women face at work and support them by removing some of the rocks. From the extensive research I have undertaken, I have distilled the many obstacles cited for mid-life women into these three key areas, which I explore in more detail in this section of the book:

- Hormonal challenges: menopause, maternity, miscarriage and monthlies (or the four Ms)
- Caring responsibilities: childcare, eldercare, and wellbeing and self-care
- Confidence at work

These particular obstacles or rocks in the rucksack can weigh women down even before they have stepped through the office door. It is the struggle of balancing these challenges with work that can stop women applying for and reaching more senior roles, or staying in the workplace altogether. By changing the system and adjusting traditional practices and policies, these rocks can be more easily discarded.

The guidance and recommendations I offer link back to the three cultural frameworks outlined in Part 2, which will help to make change happen faster: flexibility, allyship, and coaching and support.

> Businesses must fix the 'broken windows' of gender bias that impede women's careers and mar their day-to-day experiences in the workplace.
>
> *Ann Francke OBE, CEO, Chartered Management Institute*[77]

And here is a reminder of why it's time well spent:

- If you put my recommendations in place it can benefit all your employees, not just women.
- The financial benefits of more women in senior roles are proven.
- Having a diverse set of voices around the table means you are better able to respond to and represent your customer base.
- Your gender pay gap will reduce.
- You will be able to attract the best talent and put yourself ahead of your competition.
- It's the right thing to do.

The best bit is that by changing the system, and not trying to 'fix' the women, organizations will develop a truly diverse and inclusive culture where everybody benefits.

Hormone health is integral to every aspect of a woman's life, from increasing your confidence to having the energy to achieve what you want in life.

Dr Joanna Martin, Founder, One of Many

Chapter 5

Hormonal challenges – The four Ms

This chapter explores:

- ◎ symptoms of menopause and how you can provide support
- ◎ the importance of flexibility and shared parental leave when it comes to maternity
- ◎ how to recognize and support women with the often-invisible problem of miscarriage and fertility issues
- ◎ breaking the taboo of monthlies.

Hormonal challenges can hugely impact women at work and this can have a knock-on effect on others too. I have summarized these challenges as the four Ms: menopause, maternity, miscarriage and monthlies. The symptoms and side-effects of *all* of these can be debilitating and can also have a major impact on confidence levels and wellbeing. There are some women that are not adversely affected by any of the four Ms but everyone should be mindful of the challenges faced by female colleagues who may be suffering symptoms and side-effects that can potentially affect their role at work.

Although some organizations have increased health and wellbeing support offered to employees in these areas, there is still much more that can be done to support female colleagues with hormonal challenges. Seek to provide support where you can. I have no doubt that this will lead to increased retention of women in the workplace, as well as ensuring that any women who are suffering do not feel they have to deal with issues around the four Ms at work alone.

Menopause

The average age of the menopause is 51, but perimenopause – the phase leading up to the menopause when hormones start to change – can start at any age (typically between 45 and 55) and can last for up to ten years. I had no idea what perimenopause was until a few years ago, and assumed I was still years away from experiencing menopausal symptoms as I was only in my early 40s. Little did I know! Looking back, I now know I was experiencing perimenopausal symptoms. And I'm not alone. In a US study of over 1,000 women, 45% didn't know the difference between perimenopause and menopause prior to experiencing symptoms.[78] And if women don't know what's coming, how can we expect the men in our lives to know? Men are affected in different ways by women going through menopause – whether it is in their personal lives (supporting wives, sisters, mothers, friends) or in their professional lives (supporting women in their teams with their health and wellbeing).

The menopause is not just a women's issue, it is a workplace issue. Women of menopausal age are the fastest-growing demographic in the UK workforce today, so why is menopause still a taboo subject in the workplace? And why is it treated any differently from pregnancy and motherhood?

Figure 4: Menopause statistics

See Endnotes for references.

Mind the knowledge gap

The impact of the perimenopause and menopause in the workplace is huge and often underestimated. Yet [they] are still taboos in many workplaces and women are often worried about talking about their menopausal symptoms, for fear of being incorrectly judged. The most important part of the menopause in the workplace is recognising it and enabling women to be signposted to receive the right help, support and treatment.

Dr Louise Newson, Menopause Specialist and Founder of the Balance Menopause app[79]

Education around the menopause is severely lacking, although this is starting to change. In the UK it became part of the secondary school curriculum in 2020 and there has been a marked increase in media coverage, all of which is helping to raise much-needed awareness. Channel 4 is also leading the way with documentaries about the menopause and its survey of more than 4,000 women aged 45–55 who have experienced perimenopause or menopause. The survey,[80] which was analysed by the Fawcett Society, found that 44% of women said their ability to work had been affected by the menopause, 52% said they had lost confidence and one in ten women who have worked during the menopause have left due to their symptoms. Mapped on to the UK population, that would represent an estimated 333,000 women leaving their jobs due to the menopause. Eight out of ten women also said their employer hadn't shared information, trained staff, or put in place a menopause absence policy.

Around 4.5 million working women in the UK are in the 50–64 age bracket[81] – the fastest-growing economically active group – and organizations have an important role to play in offering appropriate training and support, not only for women but for all employees. Julie Dennis, Menopause in the Workplace Specialist, Menopause at Work Ltd, says: 'Conversations about menopause should be no harder than a conversation about dyslexia, bereavement or divorce.'

Those that focus on menopause in their wellbeing agenda, and provide personalized support to women that need it, will make big strides in becoming inclusive employers that are prioritizing the mental health of their staff. Providing support around menopause will help strengthen employee relations, drive recruitment and retention of key female talent, reduce the cost of absence and potential employment disputes in the future, and improve productivity. Globally, it is estimated that menopause-related productivity losses can amount to more than US$150 billion a year,[82] and, in the UK the Government Equalities Office gives a conservative estimate that absence-related costs for women that are badly affected by the menopause stands at £7.3 million per annum.[83]

It is worth noting here, especially for global organizations, that there are some countries/regions around the world that find it very difficult to talk about the menopause (or other female health issues) either for cultural or legal reasons. So, be mindful and sensitive of this if you're looking at rolling out a menopause policy or a programme.

This [menopause] is often a hidden health concern of working women, and it is so important that workers of all ages are better informed about how to confidently manage health issues such as this in their workplaces.

Dr Richard Heron, President, Faculty of Occupational Medicine[84]

Why is menopause only now hitting the headlines?

Life expectancy has increased dramatically over the course of history – in the past 100 years, the life expectancy for women has increased from 59 in 1920 to 83 in 2020.[85] On average, that is 30 years post menopause (and potentially ten before that in perimenopause), so it is no wonder that women want support in dealing with the hormone changes and sometimes debilitating symptoms that the menopause brings.

A YouGov poll of HR professionals found that 72% of firms did not have a menopause policy, 77% did not train line managers on the menopause and only 13% offered internal support groups.[86] With more women in the workplace than ever, organizations now have a social responsibility to ensure that support and guidance is available, and that menopause symptoms are being managed.

As well as being the right thing to do to support staff wellbeing and reduce the risk of losing employees, it can also result in costly employment disputes if you don't. According to data from the Menopause Experts Group, the number of tribunals related to menopause has tripled in three years.[87] Opening up the conversation about menopause and having a menopause policy or guidance notes in place can help organizations demonstrate the support provided to employees.

> Businesses that commit to [the menopause] could dramatically improve the retention rates of women in their mid to late forties and into their fifties, which is arguably when we are at our peak and most able to really influence change, drive growth and make our mark on the business world.
>
> *Vonnie Alexander, former Managing Director and Founder of Kitcatt Nohr*[88]

Mental health and wellbeing are now firmly on the agenda of many organizations, which is a great start. The next step is to look at personalizing the support offered and increasing awareness of gender-specific health problems (for example, menopause for women or male mental health). A 'one size fits all' approach won't work.

What are some of the symptoms to be aware of?

When people talk about menopause there's this huge perception that managing menopause is just about hot flushes and HRT. But there are over 50 symptoms associated with this stage… we've got 100 or so hormones running around the body and if one of those can be out of balance, they're going to cause different symptoms.

Nicki Williams, Founder and Author, Happy Hormones for Life[89]

There are many recognized menopause symptoms and every woman's experience is different. Menopausal symptoms that can affect women's work include:

- Hot flushes
- Brain fog (memory lapses and getting words muddled up)
- Sleep problems
- Low mood
- Poor concentration
- Anxiety and worry
- Dizziness
- Depression
- Joint stiffness, aches and pain
- Headaches
- Heavy periods

- Recurrent urinary tract infections
- Weight gain
- Night sweats.

Added to this, many women might not even realize that their symptoms are menopause-related, which is where the importance of education and awareness comes in.

Around a quarter of women don't experience any symptoms. However, the majority will struggle with at least one and a 25 year study by SWAN shows that Black women experience symptoms in a different (and usually more intense) way than White women[90]. Collectively, these can have a big impact on how women perform at work – forgetting people's names, meeting deadlines and making decisions. Longer term, these symptoms (without support at work) can have an enormous impact on confidence, which has a knock-on effect on promotional opportunities and sometimes the resilience to carry on at all.

> Our aim as an organization is to normalize discussion about menopause at work and provide the right information, guidance and practical support to those needing help to manage their own menopause journey.
>
> *Christine Palmer, Chief Risk Officer for Santander*[91]

The CIPD (the professional association for human resources professionals) surveyed just under 1,500 women experiencing menopause symptoms[92] – of those who were affected negatively at work, they reported the following issues:

- Nearly two thirds (65%) said they were less able to concentrate.

- More than half (58%) said they experienced more stress.
- More than half (52%) said they felt less patient with clients and colleagues.

When absent from work owing to symptoms, only a quarter of these women felt able to tell their manager the real reason. Further studies say women are more likely to speak up about their symptoms when they feel they have empathetic colleagues or managers. Rebekah Brown, founder of natural supplements company MPowder, told me that the hormone changes that women experience at this stage of life can be a bit like reverse puberty: 'To show empathy to those experiencing menopausal symptoms, it can be helpful for all of us (men and women) to reflect back on what it felt like to have hormonal changes in our teens and remember how this natural change, which often surfaced emotions that were out of our control, was sometimes difficult to deal with and understand.'

What can organizations do?

For women, it hardly seems fair that at a time when they may well be at the top of their work game, suddenly their body and mind seem to turn against them which can knock a career off track.

Julie Dennis, Menopause in the Workplace Specialist, Menopause at Work Ltd

Appreciating the number of symptoms that women can face and the impact that these can have is a good starting point for any organization.

A report by the UK government suggests managers need to acknowledge menopause as 'a natural process' (like pregnancy) so that mid-life women are freely able to request adjustments to their working conditions. This means all staff need to be aware of what the menopause means.

> Managers can find it difficult to discuss the menopause with their colleagues, due to a lack of understanding and fear they may make things worse.
>
> *Tracey Tait, Founder, The Menopause Training Company*

One in ten workplaces have menopause policies in place at the time of writing. Organizations that are putting menopause on their wellbeing agenda will be those that will win the race to gender equality. Research by Willis Towers Watson shows that 37% of companies are planning to expand provision of menopause support.[93]

> As a firm, we want to create a safe and inclusive working environment where anyone who is experiencing the menopause feels comfortable asking for the help they need to manage their symptoms.
>
> *Liz Cope, Senior D&I and Social Impact Manager, Stephenson Harwood*

Making change happen

Below are some suggestions and ways you can support the women in your organization, which are categorized by the cultural frameworks outlined in Part 2.

Why does this matter?

Don't forget! Forty-two per cent of women who are experiencing perimenopause or menopause have considered leaving their job due to how it impacts their working life. This section looks at how you can support your senior female talent, ensuring you don't lose the benefit of their experience and helping you retain women at the crucial senior level.

Flexibility

Encourage flexible hours: The freedom to work more flexible hours can make the management of menopause symptoms more bearable: for example, a woman suffering hot flushes can avoid the crowds of busy travel times, or someone who's had a poor night's sleep can start later or can rest in the day and pick up their work in the evening. Flexible hours should be the norm for all, so that those taking them don't feel hesitant, or the anomaly. As Jacqui Brassey PhD, MAfN, Chief Scientist – Director of Research Science People and Organization Performance at McKinsey & Company, explains: 'What makes the difference for women in these situations is flexibility, as this goes for many topics in life where you are juggling multiple responsibilities for personal health, family and work.'

Consider offering menopause or wellbeing leave: ASOS implemented a menopause leave policy in October 2021, offering ten days' paid leave for women suffering symptoms. Rather than menopause leave, you might consider creating 'wellbeing leave' instead, which could be accessed by anyone and would benefit those with mental or physical health challenges – hidden or otherwise.

Formalize a time-off process for medical appointments: To ensure women don't have to take annual leave to attend medical appointments, introduce a policy where they are able to book time for appointments that fall in the working day without undue process needed.

Create a flexible culture: Encourage an environment where your employees know it is OK to request to rearrange meetings where possible, to switch tasks and to take breaks. All of these measures will ensure a woman suffering from symptoms – which, let's remember, can be unpredictable – will feel comfortable structuring their working day to ensure they are at their most productive.

Allyship

Start the conversation: Sam Palmer, who founded and runs a company called Midlife Makeover, which supports women who are going through menopause transition, shared the following advice for male managers looking to support women in their teams: 'Be empathetic and ask questions such as, "What can I do to support you right now?" rather than, "Are you anxious because of your menopause?" Talk to the women in your team about how great support looks to them. Understand that the menopause affects women in very different ways – ask what they need and don't assume everyone is the same.' Laura Garside at Timpson said they encourage their managers to use the word menopause more so it becomes less of a taboo and so they feel empowered to have a conversation about it. I spoke to Zoe Latimer who is Head of Commercial Strategy at the UK Ministry of Defence about breaking the taboo. As she said to me: 'As a senior female in Defence, I can talk quite openly about the menopause and we encourage people to talk about it. It's a really different environment to where I've worked in the past. I've certainly spoken to my current female line manager about my own situation – I'm not sure I'd want to talk to a bunch of military guys about it. But in the future, why not?'

Run seminars or workshops for all employees: Think about how you can educate all of your employees, not just women of a certain age. Run events on the impacts of the menopause and what adjustments need to be made, and don't exclude younger employees and other genders. These can be a forum to share stories of different experiences of menopause: for example, a young woman who has suffered from early menopause, a man who has had experience with someone close to him, or a woman who has come out the other side and can offer words of wisdom and advice. Laura Guttfield, HR Director at Childs Farm, told me: 'We have held a series of "lunch and learn" events on the topic for the entire workforce – not just the women. It affects men too – they may know someone who is going through it or they might manage someone who is.'

Sign the Menopause Workplace Pledge: I support the work of the Menopause Workplace Pledge campaign by the Wellbeing of Women[94] where organizations commit to recognizing that menopause can be an issue in the workplace, talking openly about the menopause at work and actively supporting those affected. Employers that have signed the pledge, among many others, include AstraZeneca, Aviva, BBC, BP, KPMG UK, Lloyds Banking Group, Mastercard UK, PwC, Santander UK, Tesco and TSB.

Offer male-only information events: You may find more men attend events tailored for a male audience. This can then focus on how men can support their female employees and the women in their life, and men may feel more comfortable asking questions.

Introduce support groups: I run a virtual group coaching programme to support women experiencing perimenopause or menopause symptoms with coaching, health and wellbeing advice, access to specialists and a network of colleagues. I recently delivered this programme for Travis Perkins Plc, an organization committed to supporting their female workforce. The feedback was excellent with participants saying they are now much better placed to manage the impact of perimenopause or menopause symptoms at work. Karen Horsley, Programme Manager, Keyline Civils Specialist (part of Travis Perkins Plc), described her experience: 'This group coaching was eye-opening and really beneficial. I can already see a difference in how it is helping me at work from the things I have learnt. I feel so much more positive and, as a group of colleagues, we are really supportive to each other. It's been really emotive and I am very thankful for the opportunity to take part!' Other examples include a Menopause Café or listening circles, offering a safe space for women to support each other and share experiences.

Publicize resources: Putting resources in place that are easily accessible ensures everyone can seek out information when needed: whether it's a manager unsure of how to speak to a woman on his team suffering menopause symptoms, or a woman needing guidance on how to approach booking medical appointments.

Put a menopause policy or guidance document in place: Channel 4 have a useful publicly available policy, which may offer you guidance on where to start with your own. Some organizations find that practical guidance notes updated on a regular basis are more helpful than a policy set in stone.

Coaching and support

Encourage and pay for treatment: Consider ways to encourage women within your company to seek medical help and advice; many women going through the menopause worry about asking for time off for appointments, out of embarrassment or fear of how they may be perceived. The business could offer to pay for HRT prescriptions – as British retailer Timpson has done since

2021 – and could encourage women to request regular blood tests with their GP to check hormone levels and explore the range of treatments available to them. Childs Farm – one of the UK's leading baby and child personal care brands – has taken this one step further and pays for every woman over 40 to have a consultation with a private GP specializing in the menopause. Processes like these will ensure women feel able to access medical help, knowing it is with the support of their employer and not something they should hide.

Menopause Champions: Create Menopause Champions or Advocates who, like mental health first aiders, can signpost colleagues and managers to further support. You could also set up a menopause email address (e.g., menopause@company. com) as a first point of contact in your organization. The support they offer could range from practical advice on booking medical appointments to guidance on managing symptoms in the workplace, tailored to your own environment.

Offer coaching: Anxiety can be a side-effect of the menopause, which can have a significant impact on confidence in the workplace. Offering 1-2-1 coaching to anyone struggling with symptoms can give them the support and guidance needed to manage their symptoms alongside work.

Gain insight: In HR systems and exit interviews, add the option of 'menopause' so that you can find out if it is a reason for absences or departures (rather than it being hidden behind other reasons) and use this as a retention metric in the future.

Practical actions that can improve the working environment: Think about the practical conditions within your workplace: small changes can make a big difference to someone suffering. Some employers offer 'Workplace Adjustment Passports' so individuals' needs can be documented as they move through their career. Here are some things to consider providing:

- ⊚ Fans and good ventilation
- ⊚ Breathable, natural fibres for uniforms
- ⊚ Easily accessed toilets and showers
- ⊚ Cold drinking water
- ⊚ Period products in toilets
- ⊚ A rest area.

When requests for support are made, make sure individuals don't have to justify their reasons. If they ask for a fan, just give them a fan!

> Colleagues can claim on expenses their prescription costs when they are recommended HRT.
>
> *James Timpson, Chief Executive, Timpson*[95]

Maternity

The cost of the 'pregnancy penalty' to global GDP has been estimated at US$28 trillion.[96] This penalty causes the biggest drop-out of the workforce and nearly one in five women (17%) leave employment completely in the five years following childbirth, compared to just under one in 20 men (4%).[97]

With the advances of technology in remote working, and the amount of attention now given to diversity and inclusion, you'd think we'd be further along the path than we are in supporting women's careers alongside motherhood. We have already looked at the benefits and advantages of having more women in senior roles (see page xxi), so in this section I highlight the maternity challenges women face and how organizations can support and, in turn, retain them. Consideration should also be given to those looking at surrogacy, adoption or fostering.

I also want to acknowledge the challenges that organizations face in managing the process of maternity leave. Whether you're a small organization with one or two women on maternity leave or a large multinational with hundreds of women, I know the cost and challenge of maternity transitions can be significant. Consideration also needs to be given to the impact on those who take on extra responsibilities to cover for women who are absent. There isn't a simple answer but you might consider these two ideas. Factoring in a year's sabbatical or leave for every single employee so it becomes part of the fabric of the organization, and maternity leave becomes a piece of this puzzle. And the second idea is to create more roles that can be done as job sharing so that maternity leave can be covered by the other half of the job share.

Clearly, if organizations can support women's careers alongside family commitments for the relatively short period of time both during and after maternity leave, they will reap the benefits of retaining this considerable pool of talent in the long term.

Worryingly, it appears that women who return to employment typically see their chance of moving up the occupational ladder decrease. Women who return to the same employer risk becoming stuck in their job roles with limited career progression.

Professor Susan Harkness, School of Policy Studies at the University of Bristol[98]

Figure 5: Maternity statistics

Fewer than 1 in 5 of all new mothers follow a full-time career after maternity leave

21% of women are nervous to tell their boss they are pregnant

65% of women without children worry about what having a child will mean for their career

Only 31% of mothers return to, and remain in, full-time work five years after birth

69% say working mothers are more likely to be passed up for a new job than other employees

90% of men remain either in full-time work or self-employed in the 3 years after birth

See Endnotes for references.

Women leaving the workforce

There are still some shocking statistics about the number of women leaving the workforce after having children. Of course, there will be women that make the choice to leave the workforce in order to care full-time for their children. However, there are women that would like to continue in their careers but are prevented from doing so, due to the obstacles that currently exist. This is what this section of the book addresses.

With this as a backdrop, it is not surprising that employers need to find new and different ways of supporting women who want to return to work after having children.

I spoke to Lisa Unwin who authored the book *She's Back* to shine a light on the potential of women ready to return to professional life after a career hiatus. As she says: 'The problem is recruiters and employers seem unwilling to overlook a gap in a CV or appreciate that many women's careers don't follow straight lines.'

Why is it that women drop off the career path after having children?

Every single woman will face a unique set of challenges when taking maternity leave – and women may have a completely different experience with subsequent children. The ways in which women are impacted after having a baby cannot be underestimated: hormone changes, post-natal depression, sleep deprivation, health of the child and the mother, worries about finances, marital and other relationships, and finding the confidence to go back to work, along with other caring responsibilities and maintaining a busier household.

It is amazing how quickly people who take a career break lose confidence, question their abilities and are full of self-doubt.

Helen Cavendish, Associate Director of Research and Chief Operating Officer for Equity Research, Morgan Stanley

Over the years I have spoken to many women who have taken maternity leave, and all of them have experienced an emotional rollercoaster when heading back to work, not necessarily linked to the physical aspect of having a baby. The types of things I hear from women are linked to emotional worries and perceptions of what 'might' be:

- Will I be sidelined now I've had a baby?
- I'm not sure I want to tell my wider professional network I've had a baby in case I don't get put forward for opportunities, even though I'd like to take them.
- How will I manage if I need to leave work to pick up a sick child when my husband also works, and I don't have any other help in place?
- Will I be able to progress in my career in a part-time capacity? How can I fit work in?
- How will I ever be able to progress in my career if I'm always tired and unable to attend things like evening networking events?
- I'll never have time to do any courses to further my development as I'll be using every spare moment doing my job.
- How can I balance spending time with my child at the same time as moving further up in my career?
- How am I going to find time to connect with people and build relationships?
- If I work from home for childcare reasons, will I miss out on opportunities that are happening back in the office?
- My work isn't flexible in terms of the hours I work, and they don't trust anyone to work unless they are visibly present – either on screen or in the office. If I don't have flexibility, how can I manage the juggle?
- I'm a single mum and I need to work more than ever for financial reasons, but worry that I won't be able to cope if my baby is ill or if I'm ill.

☺ I've lost my confidence since I had my baby and not sure how I will get it back.

I am yet to meet a mother that hasn't had at least one of these concerns when considering returning to the workplace. I want to raise awareness of the challenges women face before, during and after maternity, so that organizations can start to provide much-needed emotional and practical support to counteract the concerns and potential worries that women have.

Case study: A woman's experience of managing a successful integration back into work

Pippa Begg runs the company Board Intelligence with her Co-Chief Executive, Jennifer Sundberg. Both are mothers of two children, and both still work full time on a flexible basis. Ambitious, performance-led and used to being in control, Begg found the adjustment to motherhood tricky: 'It was a journey for me as it is for everyone. Everything is outside of your control. I was very fortunate to have an amazing network and a mother who basically moved in when my husband went back to work.'

On her return, the first shock for Begg was the unexpected knock to her confidence as a result of 'doing nothing other than tending to a child, not being in the workplace and having no human interaction'. She explains: 'The business has been operating perfectly well without you, so you start to question your value. Everyone was kind, everyone was warm, I was walking back into a leadership position. Nothing had changed, yet my confidence had, and I needed to just get back into a rhythm... four to eight weeks was enough to demonstrate that I was still adding value, my brain still works.'

With a hugely talented workforce with more than 50% women at all levels, Board Intelligence strives for every woman to have the option to come back in a flexible way. For Begg herself, this meant a staggered start, with reduced hours three days a week and building back up over time to full days: 'That was great because there were so many challenges around feeding and weaning and childcare. It meant I was fully supported in that transition back to work... it is not about only doing four hours' work a day, it's about essentially being in the office shorter hours. Then in the evening the laptop comes back out again. It's an unconventional working pattern.'

Begg's advice for organizations is to keep the focus on the long term: 'The biggest problem that you need to solve is the talent drain of motherhood. When people have been working for ten years, they become experienced, they become exponentially more valuable and harder to replace. If you allow a leak in your talent pipeline, how will you ever achieve a diverse team at the top?'

What can organizations do to support women before, during and after maternity leave?

Motherhood is a pivotal point in a woman's career journey and is a time when organizations must offer support to help retain new mothers in the workplace and accept and give permission to pause.

John Pettigrew, CEO of National Grid Plc, relayed a conversation that he now has with women in his team who are about to go on maternity leave; together they discuss and agree how the employee wants to interact with the firm while they are away from their job. Pettigrew does this because of an incorrect assumption he had once made – that women would want nothing to do with work while focusing on a new baby. He now recognizes that some want to retain the connection and interaction, while others are keen to not be distracted by work. He says: 'It is about understanding and supporting those individual choices.' If you are having this conversation with women in your team, make sure they know what their statutory rights are[99] and ask them to put their choices in writing, with the proviso that things can and do change once you're actually in the full-time role of being a mother.

Making change happen

Below are some suggestions and ways you can support the women in your organization, which are categorized by the cultural frameworks outlined in Part 2.

Why does this matter?

Don't forget! US$28 trillion could be added to annual global GDP if women were to participate in the economy identically to men. This section looks at how you can support women to stay in the workforce after having a family, and thus solve the 'pregnancy penalty'.

Flexibility

Allow remote working: As a result of the pandemic, every organization now has the ability for at least some employees to work remotely if it suits both the business and the individual. Keep remote working as an option for both parents. It is also important to keep track of who is in the office to avoid the trap of a two-tier workforce: traditionally it has been mothers who end up working from home and fathers that go to offices (where the perceived opportunities are). Three proponents of gender equality – Herminia Ibarra, Julia Gillard and Tomas Chamorro-Premuzic – explain: 'If going to the office becomes a status symbol, at least among knowledge workers, our concern is that men will be gifted more exclusive or privileged access to it than women.'[100]

Make flexible and agile working the norm: Trusting your employees to do their work in a way that fits around their life will be critical in the future. For new mothers who might have had a bad night, they can have a brief rest and then carry on working when their babies are asleep if they so choose. Organizations that don't demonstrate this trust will soon lose out in the war for diverse talent.

Role-model flexibility from the top: Even if you don't enjoy working flexibly, make a conscious effort to role-model either working from home or making it public that you are leaving the office to watch a school play, pick up children from school or do some exercise. It is only by role-modelling flexibility from the top that cultural change can happen. As David Bailey, Chief Operating Officer at RBC Wealth Management, told me: 'I used to be the worst role model for hybrid working but I'm now a passionate advocate.'

Make hybrid working work: When meetings are being run both in-person and virtually, encourage all participants to use individual screens as well as a main room camera, so that those working remotely see everyone's face on an individual screen. As Ann Francke OBE, CEO of the Chartered Management Institute in the UK, describes: 'We must not pander to the people in the room and ignore the people on Zoom. Meeting technology is a real equalizer. Everybody is in the same-sized box.'

Encourage boundaries: Even though flexible working is an advantage, organizations need to encourage and role-model boundary-setting too. With an always-on culture, people's mental health can be more at risk.

Personalized offering: Every person's experience is different, and it is good to plan parental leave as a one-off prototype based on each family's needs. An experienced chef can adapt a recipe to suit a brief – the same rules apply here. Use a basic template but be prepared to tailor your agreement to the needs of the individual.

Offer time back in the office: Returners who are suffering from a lack of confidence can benefit from spending time back in the office. Jessica Chivers, CEO, The Talent Keeper Specialists and Author of *Mothers Work!*, calls this 'office osmosis': 'Having people physically around, and using Keeping In Touch days, can really help mums to get their confidence back and take the fear out of the first day.' Remember this needs to be personalized to individual circumstances.

Consider phased returns or reduced targets: In the first months of returning from maternity leave, it can help to ease the transition by building up time gradually (e.g., starting with three days a week for the first month). Where individuals have billing targets to be met, such as lawyers, consider reducing these in the first months back. It can be beneficial to think about supporting returners into more career-defining roles where they can excel and quickly build up experience that they may have missed during maternity leave, so that they can enhance skills and experience that is rewarded at promotion time. Always consider what works best for each individual though, rather than mandating it.

Allyship

Sponsor a returner: If you don't have a formal sponsorship programme in place, finding a sponsor for each female returner would be a good place to start (see pages 63 and 66).

Pass on opportunities – don't pass over: Don't assume that because someone is having a baby, they don't want to take on greater responsibilities.

Don't make assumptions: You don't know what support network a mother may have in place at home – she may be very open to new opportunities and have a partner who is happy to stay at home and look after the children. I interviewed a woman from one of the Big Four accounting firms a few years ago who explained that she had hidden the fact she had a baby from her wider network as she was scared she wouldn't be given opportunities. People often make the wrong assumptions. You might find that many mums might jump at the chance to be away from home for a night or two! Put checks and balances in place to avoid bias like this happening.

Have an open door and check in regularly: Circumstances can change from one month to the next, maybe even three or four times. Expectations of what will work best can also change. Keep the door open (virtually or otherwise) and check in regularly. Treat your employees as adults. Give them time and space to work things through in conversation and invest in those relationships.

Engage everyone in meetings: Women returning from maternity leave may feel less confident than they were before. Gently encourage participation from everyone around the table without putting them on the spot. You might also check in before a meeting to see if they have anything they'd like to raise.

Be empathetic and aware of the 'mental load': Mothers typically suffer a huge challenge around the domestic mental load. You can be a great ally in the home as well as the workplace.

Create a positive work environment for parents: Consider offering childcare services or a nursery. If all falls through with home support, welcome kids into an area of the office set up as an enclosed comfy seating area with a desk for working, and toys and books for those emergency moments. This could also be a space for women to breastfeed or express breast milk, with storage facilities.

Facilitate connections across the business: Line managers and HR teams can help women returning to reconnect with people. Brokering introductions or re-introductions can really help boost confidence for those returning to work. This is especially important when returners are coming back to a hybrid or virtual world of work.

Coaching and support

Suggest recording a video message: Jessica Chivers, CEO, The Talent Keeper Specialists and Author of *Mothers Work!*, encourages women to record a video message to themselves on their phone before they go on maternity leave, which can cover what they're most proud of, key achievements and strengths. Then when women return to work, they can play it back to themselves as a reminder of their 'professional self' and achievements before leaving.

Offer coaching: 1-2-1 or group coaching both before and after an employee goes on maternity leave can be immensely valuable. Some of the concerns and challenges that I outlined earlier in this chapter are classic examples of where someone might be suffering from 'imposter syndrome'. Offering coaching, especially if work is being done remotely, can be a very useful tool for providing support and getting the best from your returners.

Set up employee networks for parents: If your organization is large enough, consider creating an employee network for parents as a safe space to share experiences and learn from others. This is a great way for people to connect, either before or after taking a parental break, and can include tips and advice from experts on being a new parent.

Offer advice to line managers: If line managers have no experience of supporting new mothers, whether in a personal or professional capacity, offer training and advice on how to manage this type of conversation. Also, make sure that when someone returns to work that the starting point for rating performance is the same as it was before they left (e.g., if a person was 'excellent' before, they should start on 'excellent' on their return): no one should be penalized for taking a break. Another tip for line managers is to suggest that returners focus on three things that have gone well each day: this practice of gratitude is a well-known way of building confidence and can lead to an improvement in mental health.

Miscarriage and fertility issues

The pandemic has catapulted employee wellbeing to the top of the workplace agenda in many organizations. Supporting both women and men coping with miscarriage and fertility challenges would significantly advance these strategies. Pregnancy and motherhood are accepted and accommodated in the workplace (rightly so) in a way that difficulties conceiving and miscarriage are not.

Dealing with a miscarriage can be emotionally and physically draining, and so it is no surprise that women and their partners can really struggle when balancing this alongside work. Imagine if all women going through a miscarriage had the right support in place in their workplace – both practically and emotionally – how much more productive, happy and loyal they would be in the long term.

Figure 6: Miscarriage and fertility issues statistics

See Endnotes for references.

Most women don't announce pregnancies until after the 12-week scan and as miscarriages typically happen in these first 12 weeks, it is unsurprising that it is not talked about in the workplace, where there is little support available to deal with the emotional and physical effects that miscarriage brings.

Miscarriage is a private affair, and many won't want to share such personal challenges with colleagues. However, it is important for workplaces to have systems and processes in place so that employees know there is confidential support there for them if they do need to access it. For example, you might consider putting in place a step-by-step guide for employees to access if they or their partner have experienced a miscarriage: this could outline a process for letting relevant people know, how miscarriage leave works (for example, whether you need to take sick leave or whether you're entitled to other leave and whether/how that leave will be paid), access to resources and other healthcare support. Miscarriage is not something that people can prepare for, so providing employees with confidential support could help to prevent grief turning into long-term problems, like depression, anxiety or post-traumatic stress disorder. A study by Imperial College London found that 29% of women experience long-term post-traumatic stress following miscarriage, and 24% of women experience moderate to severe anxiety.[101]

Meghan, the Duchess of Sussex, in an essay in the *New York Times*, wrote that following her miscarriage she discovered that in a room of 100 women, 10–20 of them will have suffered the same loss. Yet, she says, despite the commonality, the conversation remains taboo, perpetuating 'a cycle of solitary mourning'.[102]

I spoke to the Head of Legal for a private bank, who sadly suffered a miscarriage at work. She told her boss and her PA when it happened, who were both very supportive, but because they said to others she was on sick leave, they thought she was suffering from burnout or Covid and that made her feel like she was lying:

'I wasn't sick! I was grieving,' she told me. Having had to deal with complicated paperwork involved in taking sick leave, she has since put in place plans for a miscarriage policy in her company, so that others don't have to deal with similar experiences in the future.

Fertility challenges

An often invisible and silent problem many face on the path to having a family is fertility problems: one in six heterosexual couples in the UK experience fertility challenges (approximately 3.5 million men and women of working age).[103] And there are many challenges for same-sex couples, and single people too, when it comes to aspirations of starting a family.

Those trying for a baby, who struggle to conceive and/or need fertility treatment, often experience a major impact on their emotional, physical, social and financial wellbeing. If women do not have the right sort of support at work, they may decide they can't hold down their job at the same time as managing a fertility journey. It is sad that many women often feel they must choose between trying for a baby or continuing their career. Forty per cent of women in a research study did not disclose fertility treatment to their employer due to concerns about its negative effects on career prospects.[104]

The impact on mental health can be especially significant. Approximately half of women experiencing infertility say it is the most stressful experience of their life.[105] A study carried out for Fertility Network UK found that 90% of fertility patients reported feelings of depression and 42% had felt suicidal.[106] It is not surprising that a woman's career – especially for those that don't have supportive employers – can sometimes veer off its intended path.

The additional rocks that women on a fertility journey might carry in their rucksack can include dealing with time-consuming and unpredictable appointment schedules, an impact on work performance caused by the short-term emotional and physical challenges, and potentially stepping back in a role to avoid stressful situations. None of these scenarios supports career advancement in the short term. Fertility-aware organizations ring-fence this time for women with trust and support in the short term, so that they can retain them in the long term.

How can fertility treatment and miscarriage impact women at work?

Emma Menzies, a former employment lawyer at Eversheds Sutherland and Marks & Spencer, suffered a number of miscarriages and a challenging fertility journey, before becoming a fertility at work coach and consultant. In this case study she shares her personal story, and her advice to organizations and managers on how to manage the conversation of fertility and miscarriage at work.

Case study: Managing the emotional, physical and financial impacts of fertility treatment

I was working at Marks & Spencer when my husband and I started to try for a family. We did get pregnant reasonably quickly, but unfortunately, that first pregnancy resulted in a miscarriage and thereafter we had difficulties conceiving and further miscarriages. We had many investigations, then treatment after treatment, and we were always experimenting with other forms of support and other things we could do with our diet and lifestyle, in order to try to influence the outcome. It was all-consuming – mentally, emotionally and often practically as well.

And all of this was going on alongside a high-pressure career with lots of demands on my time. Managing these two areas of my life together was one of the most difficult things I've ever had to do. I initially approached it in the same way as I had approached other challenges in my life up to this point – by pushing through and with each 'failure', working harder and harder. And after six years of that, I burnt out. That was a really difficult time, but it was also the turning point in terms of my own personal transformation, and my career transformation too.

Looking back, our fertility journey impacted absolutely everything – it infiltrated every aspect of our lives in ways that we just couldn't have anticipated.

How does miscarriage and fertility affect you physically?

There can be a lot of pain and discomfort associated with conditions connected to fertility challenges (like endometriosis, for example), as well as surgical procedures required to investigate or treat fertility issues, and drugs (including self-administered injections) required to treat fertility issues, and their side-effects. Common examples include bruising at injection sites, cramps, headaches, bloating, sleep problems, sickness, diarrhoea and hot flushes. Miscarriage can also be a physically painful experience and can sometimes require surgery, which in turn has physical implications.

How about emotionally?

It's not uncommon for people to experience depression, stress and anxiety. It builds over long periods of distress and disappointment and is often exacerbated by going through it all alone and in silence. The statistics around this are really sobering.

And financially?

Lots of people end up in the position of having to fund their own treatment at some point – if they can manage it – and it is a significant financial burden that can lead to pressure to retain or achieve a certain level of income. Meanwhile, being on a fertility journey can also cause challenges with career direction and progression and therefore earning potential. It's not uncommon for women to find themselves holding back from opportunities and staying in roles that are no longer right for them, because they think they have to wait until they've completed their fertility journey first.

Balancing fertility treatment with working

It's a real challenge to juggle a career and the 'second job' of fertility treatment. Women often think 'I need to reduce my hours, I need to change my responsibilities, or I need to leave'. They have anxieties around performance, attendance, ability to relate to colleagues and connect with work, and seeking and accepting support.

My advice for managers who may be scared about what to say

The first thing that people want is often just an acknowledgement that this is a significant and challenging thing that they're experiencing. So keep it simple and say 'I'm really sorry to hear that… that must be very difficult', or words to that effect.

After that, it's not necessary to worry too much about what to say because the best thing to do is listen. It can be a mistake to think that you must try to fix it and therefore start giving advice, making suggestions, sharing stories about what's happened to others or reeling off causes for optimism. The important thing is to listen, be curious and avoid making assumptions, judgements or comparisons.

The only question you really need to ask is 'What do you need?' and if you can help to meet their needs, then great, but be prepared for the fact that they might not know what they need immediately and it may also change, so patience and flexibility on your part will be key.

Normalizing fertility challenges, pregnancy and baby loss

Keeping the topic of fertility and baby loss silent is not helpful to anyone – those experiencing it or those employing or working alongside those who do. To normalize it, we need to talk about it, but this isn't about swinging completely the other way so that everybody feels compelled to talk about it either. It's about creating a culture of legitimate choice. Rather than stigmatizing fertility challenges and miscarriages and almost devaluing pregnancies prior to 12 weeks, we need to make it possible, and feel safe, for people to talk about these things if they want to.

We then need to be open to supporting different paths to parenthood, whatever form they might take, and however long they might take. That's the only way to make fertility and baby loss as accepted as pregnancy and maternity in the workplace.

Breaking the taboo

> I had a miscarriage in the middle of a job interview.
> I felt that I had to quietly take myself out to the
> loo and apologize to the two interviewers left in the
> room. Without them knowing what had happened,
> on my return I tried to carry on with the interview
> and made a real hash of it. I wouldn't recommend
> that experience to anybody.
>
> *Kate Griffiths-Lambeth, Transformation Expert, Group HR*
> *Director, Executive and Strategic Entrepreneur*

Miscarriage and fertility challenges are still very much taboo subjects at work, which is why it is often hard for employees to access the support they need. Meanwhile, managers remain oblivious to what's happening under their noses, or are overly dismissive of what they don't understand, or too fearful to get involved in what they feel ill-equipped to address.

Several employers – The Co-op, Monzo, ASOS, John Lewis Partnership, Vodafone and Channel 4, to name a few – have announced comprehensive miscarriage support policies. London law firm Burgess Mee has named surrogacy law specialist Natalie Sutherland as its first ever fertility officer with the aim of improving staff wellbeing.[107] The Co-op has also made its policy publicly available, so that other employers can get ideas of the support they can offer.[108]

> Baby loss at any stage in pregnancy is one of
> the most heart-breaking things any family can
> experience . . . It's fantastic to see companies
> acknowledging this impact and tackling this taboo by
> creating dedicated leave policies; this will help anyone
> who's struggling to reach out, and to feel confident
> and supported in doing so.
>
> *Jacqui Clinton, who directs Tommy's corporate Pregnancy and
> Parenting at Work service*[109]

Making change happen

So, how can organizations make small changes to bring about a ripple of support to women (and men) who may be suffering from fertility challenges and/or miscarriage? Awareness and flexibility are key. Managers need to personalize their support and be aware of what is happening for the individual at that point in time, as opposed to overlaying their own experiences or perceptions.

Below are some suggestions and ways you can support the women in your organization, which are categorized by the cultural frameworks outlined in Part 2.

Why does this matter?

Don't forget that 3.5 million men and women of working age in the UK will experience fertility challenges. This section looks at how you can support all your employees to improve staff wellbeing during this emotional time.

Flexibility

Create a flexible working environment: Be aware that miscarriage is a very personal matter: some may want the distraction of work, while others may find it overwhelming. A truly flexible workplace will ensure the needs of all can be met, through an awareness that the employer is happy to prioritize the needs of its people. Fertility journeys are also very personal and different personalities and different work environments can have an impact on whether someone wants to work as usual, work in a different way or take time off.

Introduce flexible paid leave: Miscarriage and the grief which can ensue can't be predicted, so ensure your leave policy is flexible and accessible so that those needing it can take it when they need it, without administrative hassle. Flexible paid leave can also really support women going through fertility treatment, which is also unpredictable. It can help them attend frequent appointments, often scheduled at short notice, and manage their wellbeing.

Make career planning flexible: Have a personalized and flexible approach to career planning, depending on whether someone wants to take the foot off the pedal for a short time or accelerate at speed before a baby comes along. Someone recently told me: 'Everyone's circumstances are different. It's about finding what's right for them. I've had several miscarriages and several treatment cycles, and they're never the same. What I needed each time has been different.'

Allyship

Create a culture where it's OK to talk about miscarriage and fertility issues: Give a voice to the silence – whether that is inviting people to open up and share stories of their experience or giving guidance to managers on how to have appropriate conversations.

Gauging a woman's individual needs is vital – some may prefer for colleagues to not know what they've been through to avoid workplace conversations, while others may appreciate being able to speak freely and have the ongoing support of their team.

Compile advice for managers in one place: Create a hub of information that managers can easily access so they feel confident to support women within their teams. This could cover things like what to do if a woman miscarries while at work (she will need privacy, support and potentially a taxi home or to hospital) and knowing what resources the company can offer – such as counselling and paid leave.

Be aware that the pain of miscarriage or fertility treatment 'failure' isn't over when a person returns to work: Things like due dates and an anniversary of a loss can cause future upset, as can colleagues or friends announcing pregnancies. Symptoms and complications can also continue for weeks, and even months, after a miscarriage, with many women having ongoing treatment and medical appointments.

Offer guidance on language: Women going through fertility treatment, or those that have experienced a miscarriage, might be struggling with things like sleeping, concentration, motivation, social interactions, mood swings, irritability and anxiety. Consider how you can advise managers and HR teams looking to support these women with what language to use to ensure they're sensitive:

- Being empathetic and a good listener and not using phrases like 'Don't worry, you can try again'.
- Keeping it simple – saying something like 'I'm here if you need anything. Please don't give work another thought.'
- Asking open-ended questions like 'What do you need to be supported?'
- Finding out how they'd like absence explained to colleagues and how they'll stay in touch (about recovery, not work queries).

Coaching and support

Review policies: Create and/or review miscarriage and fertility policies to ensure they cover benefits, such as reduced or alternative hours/duties, paid and/or unpaid leave for attending appointments and coping with outcomes (for those directly affected as well as partners), and financial support that can all help employees navigate the challenges around their treatment and any losses. This can also send a strong signal that you're a family-friendly employer, which will help attract and retain talent.

Offer coaching or counselling: Some organizations have free counselling and mental health services available to all employees – this can be beneficial to someone who has suffered a miscarriage or is undergoing fertility treatment or experiencing related issues. Being able to refer women to specialists where necessary is also important. Publicize how to access these resources, so those needing them can do so without asking.

Sign up to the Miscarriage Association for support and guidance: The Miscarriage Association has a wealth of resources – including helplines and online chat services – and advice on how businesses can raise awareness and break taboos around miscarriage.

Monthlies

I'm on a mission to break the taboo and bring monthlies into mainstream business conversations, so that it's OK to talk about periods at work. The following statistics give you a glimpse of how monthlies may affect women in your organization.

Figure 7: Monthlies statistics

More than 800 million girls and women between the ages of 15 and 49 are menstruating on any given day

£531 million the cost to the British economy of sick days taken related to heavy periods

1 in 5 women find painful menstruation (dysmenorrhea) interferes with their daily life

67% of women agreed they would be more honest about their symptoms with a female boss

Over 5 million sick days each year are taken by women suffering from heavy periods

46% of women aren't comfortable talking about their period as a reason for time off work

See Endnotes for references.

On top of this, women lie about their periods: many women who are affected by their period do not tell the truth about why they are unable to work, citing other reasons such as medical appointments, cold and flu or stomach bugs. There is a hidden fear that they will be penalized, or less likely to be promoted, by admitting to periods affecting their work.

> Women in the privileged West have been both covertly and overtly educated to not mention their period in a world or educational context, out of understandable fear it will be used against them.
>
> *Emma Barnett, Broadcaster and Presenter on BBC Radio 4's Woman's Hour (taken from her book* It's About Bloody Time. Period*)*[110]

Breaking the taboo

With the right leadership at the top, and an ambition to create a more open culture, we can start to change the landscape so that everyone can feel more comfortable bringing their whole selves to work.

Of course, we do need to be mindful of the fact that there are some cultures where talking about such things openly is still very much a taboo, and even women find they are unable to talk freely. However, if you can, and if you have a wife, sister, female friend or daughter, perhaps have a chat with them and find out how you can best support them when they have their period, and then think about how you can translate this across to the workplace.

> There are many barriers to dismantle. But among the most widespread and neglected are those obstacles that accompany the normal biological process of menstruation.
>
> *Brian Arbogast, Bill & Melinda Gates Foundation*[111]

There are some simple things that can be done to support women in your organization so that they can continue to be productive, even when suffering with symptoms. This is covered later in this chapter.

How do periods show up at work?

For one week out of every month, many women are affected by their period in ways that may impact their work – heavy bleeding, crippling cramps, headaches, dizziness and feeling worried or anxious, which can affect confidence levels. Some women are affected more than others and there are a lucky few who don't even notice the time of the month. John Guillebaud, Professor of Reproductive Health at University College London, says that some women describe the cramping pain as 'almost as bad as having a heart attack'.[112]

What can organizations do?

A poll of 3,000 workers by the charity Bloody Good Period found more than a quarter (27%) of workers who menstruate never felt supported by their employer when it came to menstrual health.[113] This same research found that when asked what their employer could do to help, 63% said to normalize the conversation around periods in the workplace. It seems like breaking the taboo is a good place to start when considering what adjustments need to be made in supporting the female workforce.

There has been a lot of debate around menstrual leave and many companies are now putting menstrual leave policies in place. In some Asian countries – including Japan, Indonesia, Taiwan, South Korea and certain Chinese provinces – women are allowed to stay at home for part of their monthly periods.[114] In Europe, Spain has also approved a draft bill that would make it the first country in Europe to entitle workers to up to 3 days a month paid menstrual leave.[115] However, few take advantage of it, as it can be perceived a weakness.[116] One organization that has taken this approach is Zomato, an Indian food delivery start-up: it is taking action to destigmatize menstruation and make its 5,000-person workforce feel more comfortable taking time off during monthly menstrual cycles. Deepinder Goya, Zomato's male founder and CEO, announced that anyone in the company who menstruates is eligible for up to ten days of paid 'period leave' every year.[117]

Making change happen

For me, menstrual leave is not the answer. I think a more fundamental shift is required to create an environment where women can thrive and cope not only with periods, but also with the other challenges and obstacles they face on their career journey. This will not just benefit women; it will also benefit all employees and drive a sense of inclusion rather than further exclusion and difference.

Below are some suggestions and ways you can support the women in your organization, categorized by the cultural frameworks outlined in Part 2.

Why does this matter?

Don't forget! Companies with more than 25% women on their Executive Committee have three times higher profit margins. This section looks at how you can support the women in your organization with their monthly cycles, which will ultimately result in fewer sick days and a more productive workforce.

Flexibility

Allow remote working: If remote working is normalized for all, then a woman suffering from her period will be able to work from home without anyone needing to know. She would also be able to rest if necessary, and then work again later in the day. Without the ability to work remotely, the same woman who is impacted by her period might feel she has to call in sick.

Make flexible working the norm: The increase in flexible working as a result of Covid-19 has certainly helped, as it has removed the need to raise the issue or have the conversation. Pre-Covid, I remember having a conversation with a young woman who worked as a radio producer for a major broadcasting corporation and who suffered from endometriosis (a painful period-related condition). At the time it was frowned upon to work flexibly unless you were a carer or had children. She told me: 'For health reasons, it would help to have more flexibility in terms of being able to work from home at short notice or work extra hours or days when I feel better. It doesn't seem acceptable to want flexible working for personal health reasons when you're young, but it would make me more productive overall. I would be worried about asking for it in case it affects my chance of having my contract renewed.'

Allyship

Engage men in the conversation: If you already have an allies programme, you are more likely to have a culture of open communication between men and women where things like hormonal challenges can come up in conversation. Start engaging men in the conversation and start a dialogue with the women you work with about how your organization could help. Research shows that there is a knowledge gap (unsurprisingly) in male colleagues. You hear stories of women being asked things like 'Why do you take your bag into the toilet with you?' With a little bit of knowledge sharing, these slightly awkward conversations can be minimized.

Talk openly and help break the taboo: A female respondent to the Bloody Good Period research mentioned above said: 'I think just being able to talk freely about periods would take the pressure off not only my menstrual health but mental health too. It shouldn't feel like an issue, but it does and will do, until workplaces learn to normalize periods.'

Celebrate endometriosis month: Many organizations have made the commitment to being an Endometriosis Friendly Employer and celebrate Endometriosis Month. Endometriosis is a painful long-term condition, which can lead to very severe period pain and fertility problems – it is estimated that one in ten women, from puberty to menopause, suffer from endometriosis.[118]

Coaching and support

Offer coaching: 89% of women have experienced anxiety or stress in the workplace due to their period.[119] Whether coaching is through everyday conversations with colleagues, or 1-2-1 support with a specialist, it creates a safe space for women to share concerns or challenges and help find solutions. For example, a coach can help a woman with confidence challenges that result from regular monthly bouts of anxiety. A coach can also help with the wide range of issues this presents, including confronting the fear of standing in front of a room to present, as well as tracking work performance against menstrual cycles. The key thing is listening and not judging.

Provide access to information and resources: For example, you could create a role for 'period champions', akin to mental health first-aiders, who can point people in the direction of further information or support if they need it. Or some organizations now provide free period products in toilets.

> We have recently put in place a Period Positive campaign and have signed off £45,000 per year to put period products into every one of our sites and distribution centres for our colleagues.
>
> *Chloe Howe, Head of Operations Trading & Implementation, Wickes Group Plc*

The largest barriers to women's progression in the workplace continue to arise from a conflict between current ways of organising work and caring responsibilities.

Laura Jones, Global Institute for Women's Leadership, King's College London (a Government Equalities Office report)[120]

Chapter 6

Caring responsibilities

This chapter explores:

- ◎ the motherhood penalty
- ◎ how to be an ally in the home as well as at work
- ◎ what managing the mental load means and how you can help
- ◎ the increase of eldercare and lack of workplace support
- ◎ how to prioritize health and wellbeing for your people.

D
o you know how much juggling really goes on in your colleagues' lives? When was the last time you asked if they have the support they need in order to do a productive day's work?

In 2019 I carried out research into career confidence and the path to leadership.[121] The 2,500 respondents were asked: 'Do you see any potential obstacles in your way to reaching a more senior position at work?' The second highest response was 'I worry I couldn't juggle everything in my life', which women rated higher than men (38% v 23%). Women were also more likely to feel that they 'wouldn't have enough time for family or other commitments' (33% v 19%), so are clearly more affected by their caring responsibilities than their male counterparts.

Even though we've moved on from how things were in the 1950s, it is still women who bear the greater share of caring responsibilities in the home – whether that is caring for an elderly, disabled or sick relative, looking after children or managing day-to-day household tasks. Many men have caring responsibilities too, but this section of the book is about understanding the obstacles facing women at work to progress gender equality and the reality is that caring responsibilities are not spread equally. Women account for 85% of sole carers for children and 65% of sole carers for older adults,[122] and nearly half of working-age women are providing an average of 45 hours of unpaid care every week.[123] During the pandemic, it was also women that bore the brunt of home-schooling and caring for relatives. As a result of working from home, many men are now more aware of the tasks that typically fall onto a woman's shoulders and are doing their bit to support, but it still does sit firmly in the domain of the woman in most cases.

And for some women (in the 'sandwich' generation), care extends both ways to elderly relatives and childcare. Mid-life women can often be caught between generations of family members requiring care: parents and in-laws, spouses or partners, children or grandchildren. According to the Faculty of Occupational Medicine, a quarter of women aged 50–64 have informal caring responsibilities for a sick, disabled or elderly person.[124]

For many women, the pressure of caring responsibilities is just too great to juggle alongside work and is one of the reasons why so many leave the workplace. Nearly six out of ten women (58%) say caring responsibilities have stopped them applying for promotion or a new job, and one in five (19%) have left a job because it was too hard to balance work and care.[125]

Sixty per cent of working carers in the UK have to take annual leave to carry out caring duties, taking on average six days of leave, while 30% of workers say they may have to give up work because of an unsupportive employer.[126] Fifty-three per cent of working carers also said returning to the office will make caring more challenging.[127]

Like many women, I struggle on a daily basis with the mental load that comes with managing a family. However, I am very privileged:

- I have not yet had to manage care for an elderly relative.
- I have a very supportive husband who decided to work part-time and play his part being a very present father (and took a year off when our daughter was born to enable me to continue with my career). He is also a great help when it comes to domestic chores.
- I pay for and accept help with jobs that I don't *have* to do – washing, cleaning, school lift-sharing and occasional dog walking.
- I have run my own businesses since 2007 and so have not had any added pressure to report to work at a certain time. I have never worked so hard or been as productive, but I have complete flexibility with how I juggle life and work as a central and integral part to this.

However, even with all of this, and my ability to delegate tasks (at home and at work), I still struggle as I know I am the one who has everything in my head and feel like I'm constantly juggling the many balls that being a wife and working mother entails. A few years ago, I came across Eve Rodsky's book *Fair Play*.[128] Rodsky recommends separating out tasks so that you 'own' a complete end-to-end activity: for example, one person has ownership of washing or school-related tasks. From personal experience, these small steps can make a massive difference to those with caring responsibilities. This way, I have reduced my mental load in some areas, which leaves my mind clear to focus on something else. I am also fortunate that my husband has flexibility in his work, and we can manage emergency situations relating to the children together.

Women not only need allies at work, but also at home to support with caring responsibilities. If women don't have that support, then their own health and wellbeing is also at risk.

Mid-life women who care for children, elderly relatives and manage one or more of the four Ms outlined earlier, are at the greatest risk of burnout, just at the point when they might be wanting to step into more senior roles. Therefore, it is so important to put wellbeing and self-care at the top of the agenda. Since Covid-19, many organizations have increased their focus on health and wellbeing policies, and it is imperative that this continues.

In the next section, I go into more detail on three types of caring responsibilities:

- Childcare
- Eldercare
- Wellbeing and self-care.

As with previous sections, it is through the lenses of flexibility, allyship, and coaching and support that we can create a cultural framework to support women with caring responsibilities for children and the elderly and offer them the opportunity to put in place the self-care that will allow them to thrive.

Childcare

Looking after children and a household used to be (and still is) for many women, a full-time job – and a stressful one at that. When you add a career into the mix it's not surprising that one in three women have considered downshifting their career or leaving the workforce.[129]

Managing the second shift

Women are encouraged, quite rightly, to aim high and get to the top, but all too often it is forgotten that women may have a second shift – unpaid – once they get home. At the best of times, being a mum is a challenge, and organizations can help women to manage this short period of their working lives by making small changes that will make a big impact.

For me, my professional career has had moments of challenge, but so far has been a walk in the park compared to being a mum. I remember a colleague asking how I never seemed to get stressed at work – and my reply to her: 'This is easy compared to bringing up children! I know what I'm doing at work and if there is a problem, I fix it. It doesn't always work like that at home.'

The motherhood penalty is one of the main reasons women leave the workforce. The cost of childcare is a significant factor, with research by the charity Pregnant Then Screwed finding that two thirds of families in the UK are paying the same or more for their childcare as they are for their rent or mortgage, and one in four are having to skip meals or forego fuel and heating in order to afford it.[130]

Covid-19 also impacted working mums with the additional burden of home-schooling and caring for relatives. According to the Institute of Fiscal Studies, fathers working at home (during the pandemic) managed double the amount of uninterrupted work time on average compared to mothers in the same situation.[131]

Figure 8: Childcare statistics

43%
of mums say that the cost of childcare has made them consider leaving their job, and 40% say they have had to work fewer hours because of childcare costs

1 in 7
workers had to make significant changes to their work pattern to balance work, childcare and home-schooling

72%
of both working mums and dads agree that women are penalized in their careers for starting families, while men are not

28%
of women with school-age children left the workforce to become a primary caregiver to children during the pandemic, compared to 10% of men

Only 2%
of eligible couples make use of shared parental leave

73%
of mums believe they get fewer career advancement opportunities than women who are not mothers

See Endnotes for references.

If you look at typical career journeys and expectations for men and women, I don't think there's ever been a moment in time where someone has said to the male collective 'how do you want to fit your work in around your family?' This mismatch in experience between men and women has far-reaching consequences, both in terms of how we view and value men, and the inequality we continue to see in career progression and outcomes for women.

Drew Gibson, Head of Inclusion, Belonging & Wellbeing, Santander

How do we balance things up?

Not only do we need more women in the workplace to achieve gender equality, but we also need more men in the home. Ed Miliband, author of *Go Big*, says: 'Our ambition should be to build a world where men engage equally in the caring that has historically been done by women, and in so doing reorder the values of work, family and love so that work does not always come first.'[132] There is evidence that fathers' participation in their children's lives from birth has positive, long-lasting outcomes for child development, such as improved cognitive and emotional outcomes and physical health.[133] And even though fathers now spend seven times more quality time with their kids than their fathers did with them, there is still a long way to go until we achieve parity.[134]

Yet there is still a big financial barrier that is preventing this shift. According to one study, fathers in the UK, Canada and the US were the most likely to cite financial constraints as a barrier to taking leave with their new-born or adopted child.[135]

Nordic countries are leading the way when it comes to the best parental leave policies[136] – generously paid maternity leave, comprehensive childcare and flexible working hours. The UK, despite improving legislation on parental leave, comes 28th in a ranking of family-friendly policies by UNICEF, out of 31 of the world's richest countries.[137]

In 1974, Sweden was the first country in the world to replace gender-specific maternity leave with parental leave. Fathers in Sweden currently average around 30% of all paid parental leave.[138] The government support, and the change to a use-it-or-lose-it system, has had a massive impact on take-up and maintaining a narrow gender gap; it is no surprise that Sweden is rated as having one of the world's narrowest gender gaps according to the World Economic Forum.

As well as the financial constraints which can act as a barrier to fathers taking parental leave, a wholesale cultural change is still needed. Santander participated in research which found that men would like to take more time on parental leave, but there is a fear about how it would be perceived by their line managers and their peers.[139] They also want to have more conversations with male colleagues to let them know that most of them feel the same way but are scared to say it!

Making change happen

Below are some suggestions and ways you can support the women in your organization, categorized by the cultural frameworks outlined in Part 2.

Why does this matter?

Don't forget, 61% of women look at the diversity of an employer's leadership team when deciding where to work. This section looks at how you can support women with childcare so they can stay in the workplace, progress into senior roles and ultimately advance gender equality at the top of organizations.

Flexibility

Offer flexibility and trust your staff to get the job done: 53% of stay-at-home mums say flexible working hours is an important factor in accepting a job.[140] It is important to make this common practice, so employees don't have to ask for this. As Virginia Simmons, Managing Partner UK & Ireland at McKinsey & Company, explained to me: 'The first thing we have to change is flexibility and removing the "always on" culture. There's hardly any difference between the genders on many of these issues, but there is a big difference between whether somebody has children or not.'

Set clear boundaries and trust your people: Enabling your people to set boundaries is key, especially if there is a lot of home-working involved. Encourage employees to switch off their computers and phones and make sure they don't feel like they're being 'watched' when working from home. We are at risk of e-presenteeism taking over office presenteeism and it's essential to demonstrate to your staff that you trust them. For example, make simple suggestions like 'emails don't need to be responded to out of hours'. The McKinsey *Women in the Workplace* study 2021 found that without clear boundaries, flexible work can quickly turn into 'always on' work: 'More than a third of employees feel like they need to be available for work 24/7, and almost half believe they need to work long hours to get ahead. Employees who feel this way are much more likely to be burned out and to consider leaving their companies.'[141]

Embrace real hybrid meetings: Avoid 'them and us' by setting up laptops for those in the office, so that individual faces are seen on screen as well as a meeting room 'view'. I was recently training a group where the client's tech set-up was spot on – everyone in the room had a computer screen so that those dialling in from home could see individual faces and to them, it looked like everyone was dialling in virtually. Imagine if you're the only one dialling in and seen as a large face on a screen with everyone else in a room – it doesn't make for a very inclusive approach.

Non-negotiables: Someone once told me about a system their workplace had of 'non-negotiables'. Everyone was able to put their own non-negotiables in their diary: this could be childcare related, or it could be something like a yoga class or a dog walk. There was no judgement and it was clear that each individual could ring-fence certain activities and work could not override this. This changed the culture so that non-work activities became something to be celebrated and accepted rather than frowned upon.

Don't assume parents want to work from home: Yes, everyone wants flexibility, but not everyone wants to work from home *all* of the time. Those with parental responsibilities might enjoy time in the office to get away from the challenges of childcare and the mental burden that being in the house can sometimes bring. The key here, as always, is personalization. Make sure you are flexible enough to be flexible.

Advertise all jobs as flexible: By making this clear in communications and internally, you are more likely to not only attract more women to apply, but equally retain women for longer if they are able to fit work around home life. You may even be surprised at how many men also prefer the flex approach.

Case study: Personalization – the key to helping women develop and thrive at work

Brian McNamara, CEO of GSK Consumer Healthcare (which has since demerged from GSK and become Haleon), told me that throughout his career he has seen women bow out of the general management promotion process because they either have children and they are the primary caregiver, or their spouse works and they don't have the opportunity to put their career first.

However, he shared an example of how the career choice someone makes one year can be entirely different to the choice they make in the future. Teri Lyng headed up the Quality function at GSK, hired by McNamara, and three years ago sought to reduce her working days due to personal matters. She could have resigned and left the firm, but instead McNamara and Lyng had an open and honest conversation about what she needed at that point in her career: working part-time, three days a week. Together they looked at her role, changed the organizational structure and added in different leaders to reduce her number of direct reports; this worked well. A year and a half later, Lyng's personal situation changed, the business needed her experience and skills, and she was keen to return to full-time hours. She is now in McNamara's leadership team, leading Consumer Healthcare Transformation and Sustainability – a business-critical function.

McNamara comments: 'If, at the time when Teri needed to focus away from work, we had not had that conversation, I would have lost key talent. We figured out what needed to happen to make working with us still work for her. And that can happen for anyone at any time. Why would you lose someone for their entire career instead of accommodating a shift?'

Allyship

Be a champion for shared parental leave: Make sure you are an advocate for parental leave, especially with male colleagues. Standard statutory parental leave penalizes both women and men as it conforms to outdated norms of men being the main breadwinner, which reinforces a negative cycle. The cost of childcare and the limited shared parental leave offered are very restricting factors for parents. I spoke to an HR contact at TSB, who was responsible for pushing through changes to its shared parental leave policy: all new parents are now offered a year's leave with their child, with the first 20 weeks at full pay.[142] With organizations offering such benefits to staff, it should be a lot easier for men and women to decide to take the leave.

Consider parental schedules: When looking at arranging meetings or social gatherings, always think about the commitments of your colleagues first. Is organizing drinks at 6pm the best time for socializing or could you consider a lunch instead? Talk to your team and find out what works best for them. You might find that it's not just women who find it challenging to attend work socials after work hours!

Be an ally in the home: Parents often cite 'mental load' as a burden (e.g., the 'invisible work' that covers tasks like thinking, planning and organizing a household, family and a job). Being aware of the stress this can cause and providing insights and education to all staff, with suggestions on how to support, can be helpful. It can be better to define end-to-end responsibilities rather than delegating individual tasks, so that they can be taken off to-do lists entirely. In my house, for example, my husband is responsible for our daughter's football – including kit she needs, taking her to training and matches and being on the WhatsApp group for communications. As Elaine Halligan, Director of the Parent Practice London and author of *My Child's Different*, explains: 'When we talk about parenting – the biggest mistake we can make is gender stereotyping in the workplace. Both parents have active parenting responsibilities, and it shouldn't be assumed to be just the women's domain.'

Be a role model: Men sometimes avoid making a big thing of taking time out of work for parental responsibilities, despite actually wanting to be there. This culture is starting to change, thanks in the main to the pandemic and fathers being more present in daily family life from working at home, but we need to watch that it doesn't creep back in. Be sure to make a point that you're leaving to be a parent and don't make up excuses for it. This way others will feel OK to do the same. Senior women can also role-model this behaviour. Jo Whitfield, Chief Executive of Co-op Food, publicly announced she would take four months off to help her teenage sons study for their exams.[143]

Analyse data to make informed decisions: Do you know what the take-up is of paternity or shared parental leave in your organization? What can you do to increase it? If you conduct exit interviews, how much data do you track related to each mother's situation (e.g., first or second child, single parent, etc.)? What happens to the data? How well do you promote your family-friendly policies externally? Make sure that you make the most of the information available to inform better decisions to support parents in the future.

Women can be allies to men, too: Men often say to me that they want to take on more responsibilities in the home and with childcare but are often excluded (subconsciously) – hearing comments like 'you're in *my* kitchen', or 'are you babysitting tonight?' (implying that it's a one-off event). Women should be mindful of having an open dialogue about how much both parents want to be present and what you can do to make your partner feel more included.

Stepping into different locations can be challenging. Just as women seek to be accepted and supported in the workplace, men want the same support as they arrive at the school gates.

Coaching and support

Provide empathetic leadership: With more employees working from home than ever, it is essential for line managers to be equipped with the skills to manage their teams from afar. Core coaching skills of listening and questioning can be helpful tools.

Establish a parenting group and offer parenting training: Set up a parenting employee resource group, so that parents can get together and share stories and support. You might consider bringing in speakers and offering in-depth longer-term parent training; be aware that a one-and-done training session is not going to fix anything.

Offer coaching: Coaching helps to avoid the crisis points of burnout and major mental health issues. It needs to be a continual process – maybe as part of a benefits package with budget to access a coach. If employees are coming to work without severe mental load, they will perform better and be more productive.

Provide a nursery or private space for breastfeeding: Some large organizations offer a nursery for parents to use so that mothers can continue breastfeeding easily when returning to work. If you can't offer a nursery, do consider creating a private space that mothers can use if carers want to bring the child into the office to be fed, or if they need to express milk (with access to a fridge for storage). I remember many times having to express my milk in the public toilets at a train station – not my most fond memories of motherhood!

Help with childcare costs: Provide employees with additional salary to cover childcare costs. The average British family with a two-year-old child spends 34% of their income on childcare, compared to 5% for a Swedish family;[144] it is unsurprising that many women drop out of the workforce because they just can't afford to work.

Eldercare

There are an estimated 13.6 million unpaid carers in the UK: 9.1 million of these were already caring before the pandemic, with an additional 4.5 million people providing unpaid care since the crisis began. This represents one in four people likely to be caring for someone who is older, disabled or seriously ill, up from one in six pre-pandemic.[145] With people living longer, the number of carers in the UK is set to rise even further, so this problem is not going away.

With the additional stress and strain that working carers face, it is not surprising that an estimated 600 people a day give up work altogether or reduce their hours to care.[146]

The statistics in Figure 9 are from a report by the CIPD and University of Sheffield and clearly highlight the challenges working carers experience in combining their job and caring responsibilities.[147]

Figure 9: Eldercare statistics

See Endnotes for references.

What do these statistics say about your own workforce? How many of your most valuable staff that you don't want to lose have caring responsibilities?

> It's crucial to have senior role models who champion the role of carers, talking authentically about how they combine their work and their caring because while attitudes are changing, behaviours are not.
>
> *Anne Willmot, Age Campaign Director, Business in the Community*[148]

Why are women more affected than men?

Many men have caring responsibilities too, and I am not undermining the caring work those men are doing. My objective is to outline some recommendations that will not only benefit women, but your 'caring' workforce as a whole.

However, it is a fact that there is a greater proportion of women with caring responsibilities: nearly two thirds (58%) of carers are women according to Carers UK,[149] and women have a 50:50 chance of providing unpaid care by the time they are 46. Men have the same chance by the time they are 57 – 11 years later.[150] Forty-two per cent of female carers also work part-time compared to 24% of male carers who work part-time, which is one of the reasons behind higher gender pay gaps.[151]

What does this look like in practice?

I spoke to Kate Griffiths-Lambeth, who is the former Group HR Director for a leading wealth manager. She told me about the challenges she has faced juggling the demands of a top City job, while caring for her sick mother, autistic sister and now an aunt whose health is failing. I was struck by how Kate ploughed on with her late-night travelling between Somerset and London without letting her employer know. I hope that this sort of experience can become a thing of the past.

Case study: Long-distance caring while holding down a City job

My mother went into hospital with pulmonary embolisms and came out with permanent debilitating dementia that shortened her life quite significantly. In a very short space of time, I found myself responsible for caring for my mother and my autistic sister, for whom my mother had been the carer, while holding down a demanding job in London. Work was very supportive when my mother first went into hospital, and I was able to sit and work from the hospital floor with a laptop (before the days of remote working). However, it turned out to be more complicated once it was an ongoing, permanent issue, particularly when the location was miles away from home.

Back in 2015/16 when my mother became ill, I was driving to Somerset – leaving London at 6pm and arriving by 11pm. I put labelled food in the fridge for Monday lunch, Monday supper, Tuesday lunch, Tuesday supper, ready for my autistic sister to heat up for them both. I would then drive back to London, arriving about 1am, ready to start work again at 9am. I did that for a long time, unbeknownst to my organization, until I could get things stabilized. I look back and think it was a crazy thing to do. However, I still don't see an easier solution and it felt the right response at the time.

Sadly, there was remarkably little in place at work to cater for staff needing to take time off for eldercare. The tide is now beginning to turn, because there are so many more elderly parents who are beginning to need care. Increasingly, I'm seeing men stepping into that space, as well as women. Traditionally, caring for elderly parents or young children was almost entirely the woman's domain. As I was one of the first women to join the executive committee, there was quite a lot of education required!

In my role, I did bring in mental health awareness training very rapidly followed by mental health first aiders, and 'lunch and learns' on topics such as elderly care and supporting the vulnerable – over time, it wasn't just women that attended.

I don't have regrets about how I coped with what I faced, but I wouldn't want somebody else to have to walk that same path – I'd like theirs to be easier.

Create a safe environment for carers

What is clear is that it is not possible, or indeed safe, for carers to be working and caring at the same time. Formally recognizing working carers is an important first step in becoming a 'carer-friendly' employer.

Think about this caring provision as being like a refuge on a mountainside during a storm: could you be providing a place for carers to stop, top up, refuel and take some time out to replenish before embarking again on their journey when the winds have died down? This is a better scenario than someone struggling with the challenge of eldercare, falling off the edge of that mountain, potentially harming themselves in the process and being unable to get back on the path once the storm is over.

Providing a few days' paid leave from time to time and allowing flexibility around when and how work is completed is a much better solution than the higher costs of replacing that same member of staff. A director at a major utility company reinforces this message: 'The cost of recruiting is incomparable to the cost of two or three days' emergency leave. Retaining carers through support or special leave arrangements represents a saving to the company of about £1 million per year.'[152]

Making change happen

Below are some suggestions and ways you can support the women in your organization, categorized by the cultural frameworks outlined in Part 2.

Why does this matter?

Don't forget! An estimated 600 people a day give up work altogether or reduce their hours to care. This section looks at how you can support your working carers and become a more 'carer-friendly' employer.

Flexibility

Promote flexibility but know that personalization is key: Almost half (47%) of carers are now working from home, for either some or all of the working week.[153] So, we are moving in the right direction. A personalized approach here is key as almost two-thirds (63%) of working carers say that work outside the home gave them a break from caring.

Offer unpaid or ideally paid leave specifically for carers: Research carried out by the CIPD found that one in five working carers had taken paid leave to fulfil their caring responsibilities. There was a stark gender difference: 25% of men had been able to take paid leave to provide care, compared to just 15% of women.[154] Allowing employees time off for emergencies, or other leave related to caring, is essential. If this isn't provided, carers will end up taking annual leave or personal sick leave to manage, and this will impact their own wellbeing. Aviva is an employer taking the demands of caring seriously, by offering up to 70 hours of paid leave a year for carers.[155]

Allyship

Start with your top team: Make sure you cascade the message from the top down and role-model flexibility. Showing this understanding at a senior level makes all the difference.

Offer line manager training and awareness: Offer training to your line managers so they understand some of the challenges that caring brings. One in five (19%) of working carers don't feel their line manager understands caring well.[156]

Recognize carers as part of your diversity agenda: Make an organizational commitment to accommodate and welcome carers as part of a wider diversity agenda. Many have employee resource groups set up to support in this way, but many do not.

Be aware of your colleagues' responsibilities outside of work: For example, if you know that someone in your team has to rely on other carers or help in the home, don't change locations of meetings at the last minute. Someone told me that her company would frequently shift a meeting to another part of the country at a moment's notice, which meant it was difficult for her to arrange cover. The same goes for expecting someone to prepare for a presentation using the evening before for preparation time.

Coaching and support

Put a carer policy or guidance in place: The ways in which an organization supports its carers can be documented in a carer policy. Things like in-house networking groups and employee-assistance programmes can be signposted from these guidance documents.

Offer counselling as well as coaching: Pay for employees to have counselling or coaching if you feel they need additional support. Caring brings so many additional burdens to employees and if they aren't supported, they are at higher risk of mental health challenges.

Signpost digital support and resources: Sign up your organization to become an Employer for Carers[157] (an employers' membership forum committed to working carers), which offers a wealth of information and resources to members. There are also several apps (like Jointly) that are available to support carers.[158]

Offer a Working Carer Passport scheme: A Working Carer Passport is a record which identifies a carer and sets out an offer of support, services or other benefits. Nearly three quarters (69%) of working carers said they would benefit from a Working Carer Passport.[159]

Supporting carers to remain in employment means creating an open and understanding workplace where employees can find out about the flexibility that may be available from their employer, get peer support from colleagues in a similar position and find information about practical and emotional support available outside of work.

Ian Peters, former MD of British Gas[160]

Wellbeing and self-care

The pandemic has prompted many organizations to move health and wellbeing to the top of the agenda. This is welcome news and hopefully the start of a cultural shift away from being 'always on' and overworked, which can lead to burnout.

While I focus on the effects of burnout on women, and their need for self-care (in particular those who have other caring responsibilities too), I am very mindful of the huge mental health challenges that we can all face. By putting in place some of the suggestions at the end of this chapter, you will not only be helping women manage the juggle of work and home life, but you will also be giving all your employees the support they need to be healthy, happy and productive at work.

Self-care is not an indulgence. Self-care is a discipline. It requires tough-mindedness, a deep and personal understanding of your priorities, and a respect for both yourself and the people you choose to spend your life with.

Tami Forman, Executive Director, Path Forward, and Contributor at Forbes.com[161]

On the brink of burnout

For the past 30 years, our obsession with doing more in less time has exponentially increased. We have access to an endless supply of productivity apps and devices designed to help us do just this. All this is pushing our boundaries with productivity to the extreme and starting to cause burnout. Women are reporting burnout and stress at alarming levels: 46% feel burned out, 33% have taken time off work due to mental health challenges and 39% feel comfortable disclosing mental health challenges as the reason for their absence.[162]

Burnout has now become so prevalent in the workplace that the World Health Organization updated its definition to 'a syndrome conceptualized as resulting from chronic workplace stress that has not been successfully managed': it is characterized by feelings of 'exhaustion, negative feelings about a job and reduced professional efficacy'.[163]

The impact of the pandemic and remote working hasn't helped. There's no doubt that our working paradigm has changed significantly because of Covid-19 with the necessity of virtual working, but our current approach to productivity means we are chasing even harder to achieve more.

Figure 10: Wellbeing and self-care statistics

See Endnotes for references.

What do we mean by self-care?

Self-care is the practice of consciously doing things that preserve or improve your mental or physical health. This means different things to different people, but the key word here for me is 'consciously': it implies that we must think about and prioritize self-care or it won't happen. By promoting self-care to your employees, you will not only be giving them permission to take time out of their day to practise it, but you will also make sure they don't forget!

Looking after yourself can be as simple as:

- Spending five minutes each day with your eyes closed and breathing deeply – there are many apps that offer free, simple meditations.
- Taking a 15-minute brisk walk (with or without a dog!) to stretch your legs and mind.
- Going to bed half an hour earlier and banking a good night's sleep.
- Drinking lots of water.
- Not leaving your phone next to your bed.
- Listening to favourite music or a podcast.
- Saying 'no' in a kind way to something you really don't want to do.
- Writing out a list of five things that you're great at – if you're struggling, ask a friend.
- Making something healthy to eat.
- Writing down three good things from your day, each day.

The challenge for me is always remembering to do these things when I'm busy, but even making time for one of these really helps to calm our minds.

The self-care squeeze

In order to be an effective working parent, we need radical self-care to go to the top of your priority list. You need to put your own oxygen mask on first and fill up your emotional bank account.

Elaine Halligan, Director of the Parent Practice London and Author of My Child's Different

Wellbeing and self-care is important because many women, and in particular those with other caring responsibilities, tend to put themselves last when it comes to looking after their health.

Many professional women, and especially those of the 'sandwich' generation (looking after children *and* elderly relatives), end up running on adrenalin and are in Superwoman mode most of the time. This can work for a while, but it quickly starts to take its toll as stress, anxiety and depression can seep through the cracks until one day, boom – burnout. The choice then becomes what can be dropped and often it is the career that vanishes. Things must change if we are to slow down the scarily high burnout rates and enable more mid-life women to stay in the game and fulfil their potential.

Karen Skidmore, Midlife Leadership Coach, explains one approach to managing our emotions and stress levels. For her, it's all about hormones and how men's and women's cycles differ. It is useful to recognize what works for one gender may not work for another: 'Our work and life is designed in 24-hour cycles. And yet 50% of the population don't work this way! Female hormones typically work around a 28-day cycle (our menstruation cycle), whereas male hormones typically work around a 24-hour cycle. It's not that women can't work to a 24-hour clock, but when our work culture has taught us to work in a consistent, linear way throughout the year, not taking into account our changing seasons, daylight hours or our own body's natural rhythms and hormone cycles, this is when we can burnout.'

Doing the juggle – with bubble wrap

Dannii Portsmouth, VP HR at PepsiCo, told me about this speech by Bryan Dyson, Coca-Cola's former CEO:

> You will soon understand that 'work' is a rubber ball. If you drop it, it will bounce back. But the other four balls – family, health, friends and spirit – are made of glass. If you drop one of these, they will be irrevocably scuffed, marked, nicked, damaged or even shattered. They will never be the same. You must understand that and strive for balance in your life.[164]

If work is the rubber ball, my call to employers is to provide some bubble wrap for the other four glass balls. For example, even something small like continuing to allow employees to work flexibly and minimize travel time can be a lifesaver for some.

Managing the mental load

Mental load, invisible load, hidden load, brain strain: whatever you want to call it, comes down to the same thing, which is a combination of cognitive (planning and implementing tasks) and emotional labour (looking after yours and others' emotions). I know there will be men, most likely dads, who will suffer from mental load, but it is most often associated with the daily struggles that women, usually mothers, have to manage on top of a busy workload. Leah Ruppanner, who is an Associate Professor of Sociology at the University of Melbourne and author of *Motherlands*, calls it the 'thread that brings the family into your work life'.[165]

Managing this mental load can be a challenge – I know from my own experience! I sometimes get to a breaking point where I feel like my brain is about to explode and I end up in floods of tears saying I can't cope with anything anymore (as my husband knows all too well). For me, I'm usually fine after a release of emotions and I am lucky to have an amazing support network around me. But I know that for many the stress, anxiety and depression can invade their lives in such a way that the only way out is to let something go; often, for women, this is work.

> We now have a much better, healthier workplace where we talk about work–life balance, mental health issues and wellbeing.
>
> *Alison Eddy, London Managing Partner,*
> *Irwin Mitchell*

Does working from home help women?

For some women, working from home is a godsend. However, some women can't wait to get away from the house and domestic chores, put on a smart outfit and get into the office – albeit in a more flexible way.

Being in the house and trying to work with a family around can bring many challenges as well as benefits. When you go to the office, you can physically close the door on home life and catch up again when you are back. When you're working from home, there are always interruptions and reminders of what else needs to get done on top of the day job. This burden (and mental load) is one of the reasons why women need to be more disciplined to find time for their own wellbeing.

It keeps coming back to personalization and being aware of the needs of each of your employees, so that you can best suit their working style at different points in time. For example, in the early days of motherhood a woman might prefer to work from home or work flexible hours, but equally she might be keen to leave her baby with a childminder or at a nursery to get back into the office and into a different world. Even though the pandemic has created a seismic shift in attitudes to the digital workspace, it is important to note that working from home can also bring with it other additional challenges.

> Ninety-two per cent of staff have told us they would like to do more remote working in the future and the most common request is for a blended approach of some days in both the office and at home. It will be down to the individual to choose what suits them.
>
> *Sonia Astill, Chief People Officer, Wickes Group Plc*

Making change happen

Below are some suggestions and ways you can support the women in your organization, categorized by the cultural frameworks outlined in Part 2.

Why does this matter?

Don't forget, 72% of employees rate wellbeing as their top priority. This section looks at how you can support employees with their wellbeing and self-care to be healthy, happy and productive at work.

Flexibility

Trust your people and understand what flexibility means to them: Embrace flexibility in the truest sense and allow individuals to express what flexibility means to them to enable them to live their best life. Ensure you have a clear picture of each employee's caring responsibilities and out-of-work commitments, so you can provide an appropriate set-up in whatever environment they are working in.

Scrap the long-hours culture: Wearing a 'busy badge of honour' doesn't help anyone. Reduce the expectation of being constantly available and reinforce the message that this doesn't equal commitment.

Recognize part-time working: Celebrate part-time workers, job shares and those that have compressed hours as role models to show it's a recognized path to leadership.

Don't take flexibility on holiday: If people in your team work flexibly, make sure they realize that flexible work doesn't mean working and checking emails while on holiday. It is essential that this is role-modelled from the top. If employees see managers logging in on holiday, they will assume they are meant to as well.

Encourage workplace boundaries: The advent of flexible working can mean that the lines between home and work life are more blurred than ever. Encourage employees to form and stick to clear workplace boundaries: for example, not taking the phone into your bedroom (although I know I find this tough!), shutting down your laptop and putting it in a drawer at the end of the day, taking a walk before and after work, so there is a physical door to open and close.

Allyship

Create connections: We know that social connections and relationships are essential when it comes to progressing up the path to leadership, and a lack of connection with others can cause stress, especially for the extroverts among us. With a move to more virtual working in the future, this is a real risk and something organizations need to pay particular attention to. If it doesn't happen naturally in a work setting, we need to find ways to create these connections. Sara Price, the founder of the company Actually Changing the World Ltd, which is dedicated to helping purpose-led entrepreneurs to achieve their business dreams and enhance their impact, told me: 'Connection with others releases oxytocin which calms your mind, reduces stress and allows our brains to function optimally. Trying to "push on through" without support undermines the biological systems that we have in place to help bolster our resilience!'

Be generous with your time: Whether you're a mentor or sponsor, or simply a colleague, make sure you are generous with your time. Invite someone for a coffee or a virtual catch-up without an agenda to listen, be curious and share ideas and opportunities.

Role-model actions: Give all people managers a mandate to role-model actions to support health, wellbeing and self-care, so this is led from the top e.g., taking breaks, switching off, asking for help. Someone once told me about an amazing moment in a live stream when a female director talked openly about the challenges of IVF and the decision around timing to have children; it hit a nerve with women, and they said the outpouring of support and questions was amazing.

Be an ally in the home: For those who live with others, be thoughtful of what being an ally in the home means. Be curious and ask how you can support more. Think about carving up the responsibility into end-to-end tasks. This will help to relieve some of the mental load that women can face. It might also have the added benefit of removing some nagging and to-do lists!

Coaching and support

Expand mental health and support services: Consider offering resources or training mental health first-aiders and encouraging staff to create a wellness action plan.

Offer support and hold regular check-ins: Make sure these are put in place and monitored. The more that people are working remotely, the more support and touchpoints they need.

Give additional breaks or paid leave: If an employee needs it, consider giving paid leave for wellbeing purposes. A few days off might be all someone needs to replenish and get back on the path, rather than waiting until crisis point.

Show appreciation: Ensure employees are thanked for their work regularly and that any successes are celebrated. Positive feedback goes a long way.

Offer coaching or counselling: If you think one of your staff might be suffering from mental health challenges, consider providing access to a coach or counsellor.

Prioritize self-care in a meaningful way: Consider how you can show your employees that their wellbeing is being taken seriously by the business. The healthcare company Organon announced that it would celebrate International Women's Day in 2022 by giving all staff a paid day to take care of their own health needs, or those of a woman they care about, in recognition of how women neglect their own health needs to balance the demands of home and work.[166]

> We have really focused on supporting and understanding mental health challenges and we have held webcasts with psychologists, offered coaching and frameworks to support people at all levels.
>
> *Antony Cook, Partner, PwC*

I think confidence is the key to everything. If you are constantly second-guessing yourself, and feeling constrained, then you can't do a good job. The earlier you know that confidence is a skill that can be learned the better.

Virginia Simmons, Managing Partner UK & Ireland, McKinsey & Company

Chapter 7

Confidence at work

This chapter explores:

- ◉ how workplace culture can result in women lacking in confidence more than men
- ◉ the importance of having conversations about confidence
- ◉ why confidence is important to step into more senior roles.

Put confidence at the heart of your organization

This section of the book looks at confidence in the context of the workplace. When I bring up a conversation about confidence at work, I often hear comments like: 'Confidence isn't a female thing, it affects everyone.' I agree. I don't believe that all women lack confidence or that men don't ever lack confidence. Far from it. However, there are a number of things that affect women more than men, for example a work environment that is designed for or better-suited to men, or particular personal experiences or challenges (e.g., menopause) that can cause a lack of confidence. This is what I am focusing on in this section of the book. While you can do things to support the individual confidence journey which I touch on, it is also important to remember what you can do as an organization to fix the structures and processes to create a psychologically safe place to work.

The statistics in Figure 11 are from my own research and show that confidence challenges do tend to affect women more than men in the workplace.[167]

Figure 11: Confidence at work statistics

79% of women lack confidence on a regular basis

compared to 62% of men

48% of women felt they would receive either no support or 'not enough' support from their manager in relation to a lack of confidence

compared to 36% of men

19% of women say they rarely lack confidence

compared to 32% of men

50% of women say that appearing confident, but not feeling confident, stops them from making the impact they want at work

compared to 42% of men

37% of women identified a lack of confidence and belief in their own ability as an obstacle to career progression

compared to 21% of men

46% of women say that managing a negative mindset stops them from making the impact they want at work

compared to 33% of men

See Endnotes for references.

The Female Lead's report *Women at Work: Breaking Free of the 'Unentitled Mindset'* found that women are conditioned to feel less entitled than men – at work, at home, after maternity leave, and in all areas of their lives. This leads to a lack of confidence at work, especially in negotiating pay increases, asking for flexibility and promotion.[168]

I have learned over the years that confidence is a skill that can be acquired or regained, which was one of the reasons why I set up a business to enable people to have confidence to progress at work. I personally experienced a 'rollercoaster of confidence' over my career and didn't know I could learn to be more confident until I was nearly 40! I still have to work on my lack of confidence at work (even writing this book has been a challenge beyond belief), but I now know what support I need to overcome my inner imposter feelings when they start to bubble up.

> I didn't realize you could learn confidence. It's good when you know there are things you can do to help.
>
> *Justine Zwerling, Head of Primary Markets Israel, London Stock Exchange Group*

Create a culture with less bravado and more bravery

Confidence training is not something that is typically high on an organization's agenda. When I'm asked to give a keynote talk on confidence it is usually arranged by a women's or gender network. My experience has shown that men often lack the confidence to say they lack confidence, and whenever I have done talks for mixed groups, men are happy to attend when it is positioned to help members of their team as opposed to admitting they lack confidence themselves.

Being able to admit openly that self-confidence is a skill that can be learned by everyone is a great first step. If it's not currently offered in your portfolio of training, perhaps consider it as part of your induction programmes at all levels within your organization.

> More training in confidence and public speaking would raise my profile. It would give people a better understanding of what value I add.
>
> *Rachel Mahoney, Senior HR Business Partner, Addison Lee*

There is a fine line here between not 'fixing' women and providing appropriate training that everyone can benefit from. Part of the challenge here is making it OK for men to ask for help with feeling more confident too. When I have done leadership training with groups of men and women, I tend to receive as much feedback from men reporting a boost in confidence.

If we all work together to put confidence at the heart of what we do, the benefits will flow for everyone.

Opening up the confidence conversation

Over the years I have spoken to hundreds of women about confidence, and every single one has lacked confidence at some point in their career: whether they're moving to a new role, returning from maternity leave, juggling home and work life, going through menopause or doing something with high stakes for the first time. Some women manage to hide their lack of confidence, like elegant swans frantically paddling underneath the water, to try to ensure they are not judged and at risk of not getting that next pay rise or promotion. Others simply keep quiet, put their heads down and carry on without progressing, drowning in despair or, in some cases, leave their jobs altogether.

The importance of psychological safety is important here so that everyone feels comfortable to open up when times are tough.

> Although difficult to admit, I struggle with confidence at times when it matters most. Working on my confidence has helped me take control, identify strengths and ways to manage resilience.
>
> *Jeni Thakrar, Talent and Inclusion Partner,*
> *Canada Life*

By opening up the conversation about confidence, there are several things that organizations can do to calm the waters, so that frantic paddling or drowning becomes a thing of the past. These are explored in more detail towards the end of this chapter.

How does a lack of confidence hinder career progression?

> Confidence and self-belief are key. If you are more confident, you are more front of mind for opportunities.
>
> *Helen Cavendish, Associate Director of Research and Chief*
> *Operating Officer for Equity Research, Morgan Stanley*

Feelings of being an imposter can severely impact women's career progression and in my experience, women tend to have less confidence to push themselves forward for opportunities unless they have *all* the skills and experience required.

Stepping up to a more senior role at work involves confidence in a set of skills that may not be so well used earlier on in a career journey:

- Presenting and speaking up in meetings or at events
- Networking and developing your personal brand
- Negotiating promotions, change to working practice or salary
- Communicating and having courageous conversations with multiple stakeholders
- Delegating and managing larger teams
- Pitching or selling products or services
- Holding your own when you're in the minority.

Many of these skills are taught in leadership courses, but a lot of the time employees are expected to have confidence in these skills without spending time developing them. This is when confidence issues can creep in and impact self-esteem and an ability to keep pushing forward. If organizations don't provide support and coaching around confidence and formal sponsorship, women will continue to shy away from applying for more senior roles, and organizations will continue to fall short on their gender pay gaps and miss out on the benefits of a diverse workforce.

Often people forget that confidence comes down to practice. As Louisa Jewell says in her book *Wire Your Brain for Confidence*: 'If you believe you have accomplished the task successfully in the past, you are much more likely to believe you can do it again in the future.'[169]

I often think about how our daughter, at around the age of nine, learnt how to make her first cup of tea. I remember watching and seeing her concentrate at every step of the process: making sure she didn't fill the kettle too much so she could lift it; not touching the sides as it got hot; being careful not to pour too quickly, in case she might splash and burn herself. Now she has mastered the art of tea-making (a great bonus for a Sunday morning!) and her sense of confidence means she doesn't need to think about every step in the process anymore. Giving your employees time and support to hone their skills outlined above will enable them to reach more senior levels with confidence.

Making change happen

Below are some suggestions and ways you can support the women in your organization, categorized by the cultural frameworks outlined in Part 2.

Why does this matter?

Don't forget, 79% of women and 62% of men admit they lack confidence at work on a regular basis. This section looks at how you can support all your employees with confidence challenges enabling them to perform better at work and step up to more senior-level roles.

Flexibility

Consider job shares to create confidence: Women, particularly those that are balancing caring responsibilities and a desire for career progression, can benefit greatly from job sharing to build the confidence to progress at work. Alix Ainsley job shares the role of Director of Talent & Learning at John Lewis Partnership with Charlotte Cherry, and Alix describes how working together has given them a confidence boost to progress at an accelerated pace: 'Having each other gives us a bullishness and confidence that we wouldn't have had on our own. It made us recognize the importance of our partnership.' See case study on page 40.

Encourage more flexible networking: Networking can be an enabler of confidence and is an important tool for women in progressing their careers. Encouraging and supporting networking, by ensuring you have inclusive events that everyone can attend, will enable everyone in your organization, whether they are an introvert, extrovert, male or female, to thrive. My own research found that 37% of women who would like to reach a more senior position identified a lack of visible opportunities as the biggest obstacle in progressing their career.[170]

Allyship

Put in place a formal sponsorship programme: Sponsorship is vital for women so that a tap on the shoulder is forthcoming and internal opportunities are signposted. Travel company Expedia Group has a strong commitment to promoting women internally into senior positions. Lauren von Stackelberg, its former Global Head of Inclusion & Diversity, explained: 'When it comes to getting more women into senior positions, we are trying to pull rather than push. Rather than just putting a job description out there, we ensure it uses inclusive language and work hard with sponsors internally advising on who the high potential talent is and encouraging them to apply.'

Encourage female role models to boost confidence: There is a well-known saying: 'You can't be what you can't see.' We know role-modelling has a huge impact on how men and women see their futures and the opportunities associated with this. For example, 70% of girls feel more confident about their futures after hearing from female role models.[171] John Pettigrew, CEO of National Grid, told me: 'It's incredibly impactful for women in our organization to be able to talk to, relate to and see hugely successful women at a senior level.'

Coaching and support

Increase investment in confidence training: As Robert Kiyosaki says: 'Confidence comes from discipline and training.'[172] The problem is that most organizations (and schools for that matter) don't teach it! This is why I am so passionate about encouraging organizations to provide access to training and tools and techniques when it comes to confidence. I would love for there to be a course on confidence in every induction programme, in every organization, open to everybody.

Increase access to coaching for aspiring managers: The good news is that a lack of confidence is one of the easiest things that can be addressed through coaching. My research found that 83% of employees whose organizations did not currently offer coaching and mentoring would like it to be offered. Whether this is 1-2-1 coaching, group coaching or someone internally with coaching skills, giving more employees access to a coach at the level below senior leadership is crucial in helping overcome confidence challenges when it comes to stepping up.

Give time for preparation and practice for presentations: One of the ways I learned to be more confident in speaking in front of an audience was realizing that I didn't give myself enough time to practice. This became a recurring theme as I surveyed others, noticing particularly that managers didn't give team members enough time to prepare. By being time-pressured your people can find – not surprisingly – that they lack the confidence to present. This is particularly relevant to those with caring responsibilities, who don't have the freedom to spend an evening before a presentation doing last-minute preparation.

Acknowledge that everyone lacks confidence on a first attempt: Whether you are starting a new role, talking about a new topic or writing a challenging report, a lack of confidence is completely normal when you are attempting something for the first time. As neuroscientist, Dr Stacie Grossman Bloom, says: 'We can utilise neuroscience to silence our negative inner voices and boost our confidence.'[173] Helping your team members recognize this, and allowing them the time to practise, will do a lot to boost their confidence.

Give your managers the tools to have a confidence conversation: So many women say to me that they have been told during a performance appraisal that they need to be more confident; these women then come to me with the question '*how do I become more confident?*' Over the last few years, I have delivered many keynote talks and workshops at corporate events and for organizations on The Confidence Cycle™, which is a framework I have developed on the different stages in building confidence. This can be used by managers during a coaching conversation when they are not sure what advice to give when asked 'how do I become more confident?'.

As with many of the topics covered, one of the greatest gains from tackling confidence issues within your workforce is that it benefits all: from junior staff to senior leaders, men and women. More confident employees will be happier and more productive, while women will gain the self-belief to strive for promotion and leadership roles. Confidence benefits us all, in all areas of our lives.

Part 4

Navigate your route

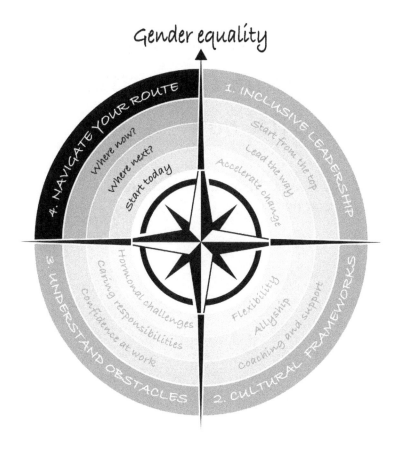

We can no longer talk about what we intend to do to make our organizations more diverse and inclusive. We must act now.

Keith Skeoch, Chairman, Investment Association[174]

Chapter 8

Take steps today towards gender equality

Where now?

You may be just starting to think about gender equality in your workplace, or you may have been grappling with it for a long time. Wherever you are on your journey, it's time for us all to take action and this final part of the book provides suggestions as to what might help you to effect change in your organization. As Marc Benioff, founder and co-CEO of Salesforce and co-author of *Trailblazer*, said: 'In the future, equality will be the key to unlocking a company's full and sustainable value. That doesn't mean it's easy to achieve. But those who fail to try will be on the wrong side of history.'[175]

Here are five steps to consider on your journey:

- ⊚ Educate yourself
- ⊚ Adapt your personal leadership style
- ⊚ Consider the culture of your organization through a gender lens
- ⊚ Understand the obstacles that women face
- ⊚ Start making change today.

The tables below provide some prompts to inspire you and some quick wins for you to try. Where are you on the journey? Where do you want to get to and by when? Who will help you get there? What needs to change for the dial to shift? What legacy do you want to leave?

> Need further advice? Book a 30-minute gender equality navigation call with me to assess where you are on your journey, identify areas to develop and what you need to accelerate change. Find out more at www.dontfixwomen.com

Educate yourself

A great first step is about educating yourself and developing an awareness of gender equality. Having read this book, hopefully you will now have a taste for it, and you will start to view things through a gender lens. The following table outlines some questions to ask yourself and some quick wins you can try.

Your own awareness

Ask yourself	Quick win to try
How often do you challenge your thinking on the topic of gender equality?	Think about attending a gender network or women's network event or experience an event where you are in a minority.
What books have you read on gender equality?	See recommended books in the Further reading and resources section, page 217.
Do you understand the obstacles that women can face at work?	Talk to your HR team about how you currently support women with obstacles (e.g., hormonal challenges, caring responsibilities etc.) and identify any gaps or improvements.
Are you aware of the specific reasons why women leave your organization?	Consider 'Stay interviews' in addition to 'Exit interviews'. This gives an opportunity to understand why someone is unhappy and respond in a way that could prevent them from leaving. Try to establish the real reasons for leaving by asking specific questions (e.g., menopause as opposed to work-life juggle).
Can you explain privilege to someone else?	Enjoy three conversations with others who may not be as privileged, or who are in a minority, and learn from their lived experiences. Pass on this learning to others.

Adapt your personal leadership style

The next thing to consider is being aware of and adapting your personal leadership style to lead a gender-balanced business: Do you want to be an inclusive leader? Do you know what an inclusive leader looks like? Are you demonstrating these traits to others in your organization? Hopefully some of the suggestions below will inspire you.

Your leadership style

Ask yourself	Quick win to try
How passionate are you about advancing gender equality? How does this passion translate into action? Do people see you as someone that champions gender equality?	Assess your inclusive leadership traits as outlined in the PACE™ framework in Part 1 to identify where you are strongest and what you need to work on. Think about how many times gender equality has been on your agenda this month. Why not ask for feedback from your D&I and gender specialists in what you can do to support them more?
How comfortable are you showing empathy and vulnerability, admitting to mistakes and having open and honest conversations when talking about diversity, equality and inclusion topics?	Think of a business issue that's challenging you and speak to a member of your team for their input, admitting you don't have the answer.

How often do you express genuine interest during conversations with women in your team?	Set aside 30 minutes to have a conversation with a woman in your team and ask about challenges or obstacles she has faced at work.
How do you hold yourself accountable for improving gender diversity and inclusion, and the speed at which progress is being made?	Can you make a public statement about your intentions for the next 12–18 months to keep yourself accountable?
Do you recognize and reward others in your team for the efforts they make towards supporting diversity and inclusion?	Check that current performance reviews recognize the effort that individuals in your team make.

Consider the culture of your organization through a gender lens

As well as thinking about your own personal leadership style, it is worth viewing the culture of your organization through a gender lens: Do you have the right frameworks and policies in place to support such a culture? Are you living and breathing your desired culture or expecting others to do this for you? By having a culture of flexibility, allyship, and coaching and support you will be on the right track.

Your organization's culture	
Ask yourself	Quick win to try
In what ways do you monitor how flexible working is balanced across your employee population?	Consider tracking remote working by gender to help avoid a potential two-tier workforce: e.g., women with parental responsibilities working from home and men in the office.
Do your employees know what being an ally to women means? Is there any training or support in place to enable everyone to become better allies to women?	Ask us to run an allies workshop using the Gender Allies Matrix™, so your employees can identify where they sit and what action they might need to take.
Do you ever feel like you may have a bias towards recruiting or sponsoring people in your own image?	Audit who you currently sponsor to check they are not too similar to you.
How inclusive are your networking events?	Try 'net-walking' to encourage extending networks and different conversations when face-to-face networking isn't always possible.
Are you aware of the benefits that coaching can bring? Does your organization have a coaching culture?	Contact me or one of my team about coaching options, and/or developing a coaching culture.

Understand the obstacles that women face

Do you understand the obstacles that women face at work, and outside of work, that impact their career? Personalization is fundamental in how you change the system to support the diversity of all your employees. Below are some suggestions of things you might try to support the women in your organization.

Your understanding of obstacles	
Ask yourself	Quick win to try
What training and support do you have in place for women around taboo topics like menopause and miscarriage?	Find out more about our virtual group coaching programmes for women experiencing symptoms from menopause or those who are affected by fertility and/or baby loss.
Does your culture support men to take an active role in caring responsibilities (childcare, eldercare or other care)?	If you offer shared parental leave, are you measuring the take-up and actively encouraging male colleagues to take it up?
Do you offer special leave for eldercare purposes?	If not, consider if this is something that could be offered.
How is employee wellbeing treated as a priority for your organization?	Consider offering coaching as a way to support those that are struggling with wellbeing issues.
Do you know how to support your employees to overcome confidence challenges?	Why not ask me to deliver a keynote talk or workshop on 'How to excel in your career with confidence'?

Start making changes today

Women can't wait any longer for change to happen. It must start today. This is not a nice-to-have piece of work to put off to next quarter or next year. This is today's priority and collectively we can make change happen.

Your actions

Ask yourself	Quick win to try
What steps are you personally taking to achieve gender equality? How are your actions perceived by others? What legacy do you want to leave?	Reflect on what gender objectives you want to achieve in the next three years. Ask your colleagues for their input on this, and to keep you accountable.
How does gender appear on your dashboard of business priorities?	Start adding gender to your daily agenda and your list of business priorities.
When did you last use your position and power to stand up for gender equality?	Can you find an opportunity to talk to and influence your peers about what they're doing in this space?
Do you hear yourself making excuses about how long particular initiatives may take to create an impact?	Can you set some new milestones for change to happen more quickly? What is stopping progress?
Do you have the right team around you to achieve your gender objectives? How do you encourage and reward inclusive behaviours in your organization?	Think about modifying performance reviews to recognize and reward the effort that individuals make. Buy copies of this book to inspire your team!

These tables are available as a free download so you can share them as a gender equality checklist with others in your organization. See www.dontfixwomen.com

Where next?

This book has explored and analyzed why gender equality is important, why it can't wait, why we need to fix the system rather than the women, why there are so many obstacles still in the way and what you can do to make change happen.

If you or your colleagues need support as you navigate the path to gender equality, please do get in touch. I'd be delighted to help you shine a light on what you can do to create a more balanced workplace in the future. Book a 30-minute gender equality navigation call with me to assess where you are on your journey, identify areas to develop and what you need to accelerate change.

Find out more at **www.dontfixwomen.com**

A final word

This book has outlined how gender equality is not about fixing women, but about improving and adapting our organizations to become places where all employees can thrive. Now you have the strategies and tools in your leadership kitbag, you can start implementing small steps today to create more gender-balanced businesses in the future.

By taking personal responsibility for challenging gender stereotypes, checking your personal biases, understanding your privilege, and role-modelling inclusive behaviours at work and in the home, you will move the compass needle north to gender equality.

Let's change the narrative in the organizations where we work and in the homes that we run. Let girls and boys grow up to be whatever they want to be, whether that's a CEO or a stay-at-home parent, without anything holding them back: wouldn't that be a great legacy to leave?

Together we can create a better future for all.

Need support as you navigate your path to gender equality?

Start today

My mission at *Encompass Equality* is to champion gender equality and drive forward strategies for the retention of women in the workplace. We achieve this through coaching, training, consulting and research, and act as gender equality partners to leading organizations.

If you or your colleagues are looking for inspiration and solutions as you navigate the path to gender equality, my team and I are here to help. Please visit www.dontfixwomen.com to:

- ⊚ **Download** free resources and tools outlined in this book, including the helpful navigation tables in Part 4 (which provide prompts to inspire you and some quick wins to try), and a *Top Tips* handbook.
- ⊚ **Schedule** a 30-minute gender equality navigation call with me or a member of my team to assess where you are on your journey, identify areas to develop and what you need to accelerate change.
- ⊚ **Sign up** for monthly inspiration and updates on the topic of gender equality.
- ⊚ **Book** a keynote talk on the topics covered in this book.
- ⊚ **Buy** discounted copies of this book to share with your colleagues. We can introduce new case studies, customize the content and co-brand your copies to suit your business's needs.

Through our extensive research and work with future-thinking organizations, we provide inspiration, guidance and support to give you the confidence to make big change happen.

Organizations	Leaders	Employees
Inspiration and advice to develop cultural frameworks to change the system, not 'fix' the women.	*Guidance* to help navigate your route to gender equality by embedding inclusive leadership traits.	*Support* in raising awareness of the obstacles that women face at work and how to overcome them.

Continue the conversation at
www.dontfixwomen.com
www.encompassequality.com

 Joy Burnford

 Joy Burnford @Forbes

 The Confidence Conversation podcast with Joy Burnford

 hello@encompassequality.com

About the author

Joy Burnford advises clients on how to navigate the path to gender equality by driving forward strategies for the retention of women. She is founder and CEO of *Encompass Equality* (formerly *My Confidence Matters*), and is a recognized trailblazer in gender equality with over 25 years' experience as a business leader and entrepreneur.

As host of 'The Confidence Conversation' podcast and author of more than 70 articles on Forbes.com, she has interviewed hundreds of senior business leaders, board members, CEOs, authors and experts, and has been cited in national, business and HR press.

Through her extensive research, she helps build awareness and understanding of the obstacles that women face at work and provides bespoke practical tools and frameworks to make big change happen. She and her team deliver talks, workshops, coaching and leadership programmes for both women and men. Joy regularly speaks at conferences and industry events and is working with the British Standards Institution to create a new standard for menopause and menstruation in the workplace.

Joy is a Non-Executive Director and Vice-President of the East of England Co-op, playing a key role in ensuring the long-term success of the business, shaping future direction and overseeing governance, policy and strategy decisions.

She is a member of the Women's Equality Party and an active supporter of the *Unleashed Women* campaign led by the Hunger Project UK charity whose mission is to end hunger and poverty by pioneering women-centred strategies (www.thehungerproject.org.uk/unleashedwomen).

Joy is a busy wife and mum to two wonderfully different children and a puppy called Ziggy, and so understands the challenges that many women face on a daily basis!

Continue the conversation and share the impact you are making at www.dontfixwomen.com

Acknowledgements

I knew it was the right time to write this book, but when it came to it, I knew I couldn't do it alone. I am so thankful for the amazing team of people around me that have helped to make this happen.

For my brilliant book team:

- My publisher, Alison Jones, who has been an inspiration, mentor and coach. From her business book proposal challenge to keeping me enthused and on track along the way, her unwavering belief in me gave me the confidence to become an author. Her weekly 'campfire' provided essential tools and a support network of like-minded authors, many of whom I now call friends.
- Claire Dagwell for her continual support with everything book related – research, planning, design, writing, editing,

challenge and motivation to keep me going when I didn't think I could do it.

@ My beta readers who spent time reading through the manuscript and providing comments to help shape the book and in particular my Strategy Director, Edward Haigh.

@ Lucy Hutchings for finessing my words.

@ Alexia Padgham for arranging hundreds of book interviews and for always anticipating what I need before I realize myself.

@ Lily Horseman for working with me in her unique way to produce her wonderful 'in-the-moment' illustrations.

@ Kirsten Buckle for her creative graphic design and technical wizardry.

@ Sophie Robinson and the editorial and design team at Newgen for refining my manuscript and bearing with me over the multiple edits of the cover design!

For my supportive family:

@ My husband, Andy, who is a role model ally in the home and who takes on an equal share of our parenting responsibilities to enable me to do the work I do.

@ My children for seeing a life of possibilities ahead of them, inspiring me to make change happen in their lifetime and for being patient with me when I am working.

@ My own mother, Sue Peterson, who has been my role model – always encouraging me, never letting stereotypes enter my world as a child, and giving me every opportunity possible when I was growing up.

@ My puppy, Ziggy, who woke me up for months at 5am, which helped me find my rhythm of writing before everyone in the house woke up and the day job kicked off!

For my friends and work colleagues, too many to mention individually, for keeping me grounded and sane. On dog walks, during chats over coffee and Zoom calls, they have all listened when juggling work and life was tough.

I would like to thank all the incredible people I interviewed and talked to during the process of researching this book. Your insights, inspiration and words of wisdom shine through these pages.

Corporate viewpoints

- Alix Ainsley, Director of Talent & Learning, John Lewis Partnership
- Helen Ashton, former ASOS Chief Financial Officer, Non-Executive Director at JD Sports, and Founder of Retail Consultancy, Shape Beyond
- Sonia Astill, Chief People Officer, Wickes Group Plc
- Meerah Azhar, Vice President, Payments Product Strategy and Insights, JP Morgan
- David Bailey, Chief Operating Officer, RBC Wealth Management
- James Bailey, Executive Director, Waitrose (John Lewis Partnership)
- Julie Baker, Head of Enterprise, Climate Engagement and Partnerships, NatWest Group
- Annie Baxter, Chief of Staff, PwC
- Pippa Begg, Co-Chief Executive, Board Intelligence
- Annabel Bosman, Managing Director, RBC Wealth Management
- Caroline Bowes, Director, Human Resources EMEA, Dechert LLP
- Tamara Box, Managing Partner EME, Reed Smith LLP
- Calum Brewster, CEO, Brown Shipley
- Phil Burgess, Chief People Officer, C Space
- Helen Buttery, Lead HR Business Partner, Wickes Group Plc
- Justine Campbell, Managing Partner for Talent, EY
- Margaret Campbell, Partner, Reed Smith LLP
- Helen Cavendish, Associate Director of Research and Chief Operating Officer for Equity Research, Morgan Stanley

- Nicholas Cheffings, Senior Counsel and former Global Chair, Hogan Lovells
- Charlotte Cherry, Director of Talent & Learning, John Lewis Partnership
- Sarah Churchman OBE, Chief Inclusion, Community & Wellbeing Officer, PwC
- James Clarry, Chief Operating Officer, Coutts and the Wealth Businesses of The NatWest Group
- Nathan Coe, CEO, Auto Trader Group Plc
- Georgina Collins, Global Chief Talent Officer, Interbrand
- Julie Collins Powell, Test Lead, Rathbone Group Plc
- Antony Cook, Partner, PwC
- Liz Cope, Senior D&I and Social Impact Manager, Stephenson Harwood
- Caroline Cryer, Global Head of Talent and Capability, GSK Consumer Healthcare (which has since demerged from GSK and become Haleon)
- David Dunckley, CEO, Grant Thornton UK LLP
- Alison Eddy, London Managing Partner, Irwin Mitchell
- Doug Field OBE, Joint CEO, East of England Co-op
- Shona Fleming, Chief Executive, ScotsCare and Borderline
- Emily Franklin, People Partner, Kaluza (formerly at TSB)
- Laura Garside, Colleague Support Advisor, Timpson
- Sayeh Ghanbari, Partner, EY
- Drew Gibson, Head of Inclusion, Belonging & Wellbeing, Santander
- Bethan Gill, Associate Director, Inclusion & Diversity, Grant Thornton UK LLP
- Laura Guttfield, formerly HR Director, Childs Farm
- Karen Horsley, Programme Manager, Keyline Civils Specialist (part of Travis Perkins Plc)
- Chloe Howe, Head of Operations Trading & Implementation, Wickes Group Plc
- Donna Kennedy, Global Director of People and Culture, X4 Group
- Gary Kibble, Chief Marketing Officer, Wickes Group Plc

- Jennie Koo, Head of Operations Risk Management, Capital One and Management Board of Women in Banking and Finance
- Rachel Macfarlane, Group Head of Legal, Quintet Private Bank
- Rachel Mahoney, Senior HR Business Partner, Addison Lee
- Gary Manning, Head of People, Digital Surgery/Touch Surgery, Medtronic
- Imogen Marouillat, Project Associate Director, Merck Group
- David Mash, Senior HR Business Partner, Wickes Group Plc
- Will McDonald, former Group Sustainability and Public Policy Director, Aviva Plc and Chair of Trustees at The Fatherhood Institute
- Jennifer McGrandle, Employment Lawyer, Dechert LLP
- Brian McNamara, CEO, GSK Consumer Healthcare (which has since demerged from GSK and become Haleon)
- Rhia Mitchell, Executive Communications Director, GSK Consumer Healthcare (which has since demerged from GSK and become Haleon)
- Frank Moxon, Senior Independent Director, Jersey Oil & Gas Plc, and Past Master, Worshipful Company of International Bankers
- Cristina Ortega Duran, Chief Digital Health Officer and Board Member, AstraZeneca
- John Pettigrew, CEO, National Grid
- Dannii Portsmouth, Vice President of Human Resources, PepsiCo
- Sian Prigg, Senior Learning and Talent Manager, Opel Vauxhall Finance, and Founder of Start Sooner
- Justina Rhodes, Head of Portfolio Management Office, Gallagher
- Laura Riddeck, Counsel, Reed Smith LLP
- Emma Rose, Chief Human Resources Officer, Travis Perkins Plc

- Parv Sangera, Managing Director, The Bathroom Showroom, Highbourne Group
- David Schwimmer, CEO, London Stock Exchange Group
- Virginia Simmons, Managing Partner UK & Ireland, McKinsey & Company
- Jeni Thakrar, Talent and Inclusion Partner, Canada Life
- Claire Valoti, Vice President EMEA, Snap Inc
- Lauren von Stackelberg, Chief Diversity & Inclusion Officer, The LEGO Group
- Anita Walters, HR Leader and Executive Coach, Aviva Plc
- Lin Yue, Executive Director, Goldman Sachs Asset Management
- Justine Zwerling, Head of Primary Markets Israel, London Stock Exchange Group

Gender equality viewpoints

- Jacqueline Abbott-Deane, CEO, One Loud Voice for Women
- Hamish Adamson, Gender Ally Group, HM Government
- Laura Aiken, Consultant and DEI Specialist, Kintla
- Lauren Alani, Healthcare Businesswomen's Association
- Olivia Bath, Founder, The Women's Vault
- Professor Rosie Campbell, Director, The Global Institute for Women's Leadership at King's College London
- Fiona Dawson CBE, Chair, UK Women's Business Council
- Edwina Dunn OBE, Founder, The Female Lead
- Jodie Evans, OSM Commercial Manager and Defence Women's Network Lead, UK Ministry of Defence
- Ann Francke OBE, CEO, Chartered Management Institute UK
- Simon Gallow, Advocate and HeForShe Lead, UN Women UK
- Tamara Gillan, Founder, The WealthiHer Network

- Fiona Hathorn, CEO, Women on Boards UK
- Sarah Le Breton, Gender Consultant, Advocate, Writer and Researcher
- Joanne Lockwood, Founder and CEO, Inclusion & Belonging Specialist, See Change Happen
- Marie Manley, Customer Operations Specialist, See Change Happen
- Baroness Helena Morrissey DBE, Financier, Author and Campaigner
- Professor Helen Pankhurst CBE
- Anna Richards, Head of Communications and Marketing, WorkLife Central (formerly Cityparents)
- Belinda Riley, Diversity, Equity and Inclusion Consultant
- Mark Robinson OBE, Former Head Coach of England Women's Cricket
- Kathrin Schoeorn, Board Member, Healthcare Businesswomen's Association
- Lisa Unwin, Co-Founder and CEO, Reignite Academy, and Author of *She's Back*
- Vanessa Vallely OBE, Founder and CEO, WeAreTheCity and WeAreTechWomen
- Gill Whitty-Collins, Author of *Why Men Win at Work*
- Denise Wilson OBE, CEO, FTSE Women Leaders Review
- Avivah Wittenberg-Cox, CEO, 20-first, and Author of several books including *Seven Steps to Leading a Gender Balanced Business* and *Why Women Mean Business*

Expert viewpoints

- Shiona Adamson, Director of Communications, Change and Engagement, Government Communication Service
- Stephanie Aitken, Women's Coach & Trainer, Stephanie Aitken Coaching
- Kate Bassett, Financial Times

- Helen Beedham, Director, Helen Beedham Consulting Ltd, and Author of *The Future of Time*
- Katie Biddiss, Clinic Director, The Surrey Park Clinic
- Jacqui Brassey PhD, MAfN, Chief Scientist – Director of Research Science People and Organization Performance, McKinsey & Company, Affiliated Senior Expert, McKinsey Health Institute, Fellow Researcher, VU Amsterdam, Adjunct Professor, IE University Madrid and Supervisory Board Member, Save the Children NL
- Rebekah Brown, Founder, MPowder
- Sarah Burgess, Business Development Consultant
- Jessica Chivers, CEO, The Talent Keeper Specialists and Author of *Mothers Work!*
- Helena Clayton, Leadership Development Consultant and Coach
- Lois Dabrowski, HR Marketing Specialist
- Julie Dennis, Menopause in the Workplace Specialist, Menopause at Work Ltd
- Ruth Devlin, Founder, Let's Talk Menopause, and Author of *Men: Let's Talk Menopause*
- Caroline Doherty, Managing Director, Capability Jane Recruitment Ltd
- Caroline Gosling, Director, Culture & Engagement, Rubica
- Kate Griffiths-Lambeth, Transformation Expert, Group HR Director, Executive and Strategic Entrepreneur
- Helen Grimshaw, Co-Founder, Elana
- Elaine Halligan, Director, Parent Practice London and Author of *My Child's Different*
- Helena Holrick, Chief Cheerleader, Helping You Shine, and Co-Founder, Speaker INsight
- Jane Johnson, Founder, Careering into Motherhood
- Timea Kristof, Chief Disruptor & Head of Executive Coaching, Gekko Consulting
- Manda Lakhani, Board Trustee, The Hunger Project UK

- Zoe Latimer, Head of Commercial Strategy, UK Ministry of Defence
- Dr Joanna Martin, Founder, One of Many
- Debra Mashek, Collaboration Advisor and Author of *Collabor(h)ate*
- Emma Menzies, Fertility at Work Coach, Ready Steady Coach
- Sam Palmer, Founder, Midlife Makeover
- Richard Pickard, CEO, Inclusive Search
- Sara Price, Founder, Actually Changing the World Ltd
- Penny Pullan, Director, Making Projects Work Ltd, and Author of *Virtual Leadership: Practical Strategies for Success with Remote or Hybrid Work and Teams*
- Katherine Ray, Founder and Director, Talentology Ltd
- Alice Sheldon, Founder, Needs Understanding, and Author of *Why Weren't We Taught This at School?*
- Karen Skidmore, Midlife Leadership Coach, Business Strategist and Author of *True Profit Business*
- Erica Stocks MBA, Director, Fairway Coaching Consultancy
- Tracey Tait, Founder, The Menopause Training Company
- Charmian Tardieu, Insights & Strategy Consultant and Executive Coach, MilesFurther
- Sarah Tennant, Co-Founder and Director, Coach Matters
- Helen Tupper, Co-Founder, Amazing If, and Co-Author of *The Squiggly Career* and *You Coach You*
- Lilian Ugwumadu, Consultant Gynaecologist, The Surrey Park Clinic
- Kathryn Wakefield, Executive Coach and Facilitator
- Catherine Weetman, Author of *A Circular Economy Handbook* and Strategic Advisor
- Chris Williams, Leadership Coach
- Nicki Williams, Founder and Author, Happy Hormones for Life
- Victoria Winkler, Director of Professional Development, CIPD

Further reading and resources

Organizations and networks

- Bayes Business School www.bayes.city.ac.uk
- British Standards Institution (BSI) www.bsigroup.com
- Business In The Community (BITC) www.bitc.org.uk
- Capability Jane Recruitment Ltd www.capabilityjane.com
- Chartered Institute of Personnel and Development (CIPD) www.cipd.co.uk
- Encompass Equality www.encompassequality.com
- Fawcett Society www.fawcettsociety.org.uk
- FTSE Women Leaders www.ftsewomenleaders.com
- Global Institute for Women's Leadership www.kcl.ac.uk/giwl
- Government Equalities Office www.gov.uk/government/organisations/government-equalities-office
- HeForShe www.heforshe.org
- Inspiring Girls International www.inspiring-girls.com
- The International Coaching Federation www.coachingfederation.org
- McKinsey & Company www.mckinsey.com
- One Loud Voice www.oneloudvoice.co.uk
- Tech She Can www.techshecan.org
- The Female Lead www.thefemalelead.com
- Timewise www.timewise.co.uk
- UN Women www.unwomen.org
- WeAreTheCity www.wearethecity.com
- Women on Boards www.womenonboards.net
- World Economic Forum www.weforum.org

Books

Emma Barnett, *It's About Bloody Time. Period.* 2021, HarperCollins Publishers.

Helen Beedham, *The Future of Time: How 're-working' time can help you boost productivity, diversity and wellbeing.* 2022, Practical Inspiration Publishing.

Marc Benioff and Monica Langley, *Trailblazer: The Power of Business as the Greatest Platform for Change.* 2020, Simon & Schuster.

Tomas Chamorro-Premuzic, *Why Do So Many Incompetent Men Become Leaders? (And How to Fix It).* 2019, Harvard Business Review Press.

Caroline Criado-Perez, *Invisible Women: Exposing Data Bias in a World Designed for Men.* 2020, Vintage Publishing.

Ann Francke, *Create a Gender-Balanced Workplace.* 2019, Penguin Books Ltd.

Alison Hardingham, *The Coach's Coach: Personal Development for Personal Developers.* 2004, Chartered Institute of Personnel & Development.

Louisa Jewell, *Wire Your Brain for Confidence: The Science of Conquering Self-Doubt.* 2017, Famous Warrior Press.

Kate Lanz and Paul Brown, *All the Brains in the Business: The Engendered Brain in the 21st Century Organisation – The Neuroscience of Business.* 2020, Springer Nature Switzerland AG.

Ed Miliband, *Go Big: How to Fix Our World.* 2021, Vintage Publishing.

Julia Muir, *Change the Game: The Leader's Route Map to a Winning, Gender-balanced Business.* 2021, Practical Inspiration Publishing.

Patricia Pulliam Phillips, Jack J. Phillips and Lisa Ann Edwards, *Measuring the Success of Coaching: A Step-by-Step Guide for Measuring*

Impact and Calculating ROI. 2012, American Society for Training & Development.

Jane Renton, *Coaching and Mentoring: What They Are and How to Make the Most of Them.* 2009, Bloomberg Press.

Eve Rodsky, *Fair Play: Share the Mental Load, Rebalance Your Relationship and Transform Your Life.* 2021, Quercus Publishing.

Mary Ann Sieghart, *The Authority Gap.* 2022, Transworld Publishers Ltd.

David G. Smith and W. Brad Johnson, *Good Guys: How Men Can Be Better Allies for Women in the Workplace.* 2020, Harvard Business Review Press.

Helen Tupper and Sarah Ellis, *You Coach You: How to Overcome Challenges and Take Control of Your Career.* 2022, Penguin Books Ltd.

Sir John Whitmore, *Coaching for Performance: The Principles and Practice of Coaching and Leadership.* 2009, John Murray Press.

Gill Whitty-Collins, *Why Men Win at Work: ... and How We Can Make Inequality History.* 2021, Luath Press Ltd.

Avivah Wittenberg-Cox and Alison Maitland, *Why Women Mean Business: Understanding the Emergence of our Next Economic Revolution.* 2009, John Wiley & Sons Inc.

Caring resources

- Carers UK www.carersuk.org
- Employers for Carers www.employersforcarers.org
- Jointly www.jointlyapp.com
- Mind www.mind.org.uk
- NHS Live Well www.nhs.uk/live-well
- WorkLife Central (formerly Cityparents) www.worklifecentral.com

Menopause and monthlies resources

- Channel 4 menopause resources www.channel4.com/press/news/world-menopause-day-2021
- Daisy Network www.daisynetwork.org
- Faculty of Occupational Medicine www.fom.ac.uk
- GenM Invisibility Report www.gen-m.com/insight
- Happy Hormones for Life (Nicki Williams) www.happyhormonesforlife.com
- Louise Newson www.newsonhealth.co.uk
- MegsMenopause www.megsmenopause.com
- Menopause Café www.menopausecafe.net
- Menopause in the Workplace www.menopauseintheworkplace.co.uk
- Menopause Matters www.menopausematters.co.uk
- Menopause Training Company www.menopausetrainingcompany.com
- Mental Health First Aid England www.mhfaengland.org
- Over The Bloody Moon www.overthebloodymoon.com
- Peppy www.peppy.health
- The Menopause Charity www.themenopausecharity.org
- The Surrey Park Clinic www.thesurreyparkclinic.co.uk

Miscarriage and fertility resources

- Fertifa and Workplace Fertility Community www.fertifa.com
- Fertility Network UK www.fertilitynetworkuk.org
- Miscarriage Association www.miscarriageassociation.org.uk
- Peppy www.peppy.health
- Ready Steady Coach (Emma Menzies) www.readysteadycoach.com
- The Surrey Park Clinic www.thesurreyparkclinic.co.uk
- Tommy's www.tommys.org

Please also see the Endnotes.

Endnotes

[1] https://abcnews.go.com/blogs/headlines/2014/02/heres-a-list-of-58-gender-options-for-facebook-users

Introduction

[2] www.weforum.org/reports/global-gender-gap-report-2021/digest

[3] https://execpipeline.com/wp-content/uploads/2021/07/Women-Count-2021-Report.pdf

[4] www.spencerstuart.com/research-and-insight/uk-board-index/diversity

[5] www.hrzone.com/community/blogs/gfreynolds/average-employee-costs-smes-ps11000-to-replace

[6] www.pwc.com/gx/en/about/diversity/iwd/iwd-female-talent-report-web.pdf

[7] https://ftsewomenleaders.com/

[8] https://25x25.uk/

[9] Avivah Wittenberg-Cox and Alison Maitland, *Why Women Mean Business: Understanding the Emergence of our Next Economic Revolution*, John Wiley & Sons, p. 20.

[10] www.ons.gov.uk/employmentandlabourmarket/peopleinwork/earningsandworkinghours/bulletins/genderpaygapintheuk/2021

[11] www.kcl.ac.uk/news/uk-gender-pay-gap-reporting-has-no-teeth

Part 1: Inclusive leadership

[12] www2.deloitte.com/global/en/pages/about-deloitte/articles/women-at-work-global-outlook.html

[13] www.pwc.com/gx/en/ceo-agenda/ceosurvey/2022.html

[14] www.forbes.com/sites/deloitte/2021/07/01/why-women-are-leaving-the-workforce-after-the-pandemic-and-how-to-win-them-back/?sh=4e8a9a55796e

[15] www.bitc.org.uk/wp-content/uploads/2020/08/bitc-report-gender-ttt50supplement-july20.pdf

[16] www.managers.org.uk/about-cmi/media-centre/press-office/press-releases/women-remain-underrepresented-in-senior-and-strategic-management-positions-research-shows/

[17] https://25x25.uk/our-framework/

[18] Marc Benioff and Monica Langley, *Trailblazer: The Power of Business as the Greatest Platform for Change*, Simon & Schuster, p. 103.

[19] www.bayes.city.ac.uk/about/more/diversity-equity-and-inclusion/global-womens-leadership/events

[20] www.mckinsey.com/featured-insights/diversity-and-inclusion/women-in-the-workplace

[21] www.managers.org.uk/knowledge-and-insights/research-thought-leadership/management-transformed/

[22] www.karianandbox.com/insight/4/the-essential-guide-to-engaging-and-enabling-employees-in-a-crisis

[23] www.ey.com/en_gl/women-fast-forward/why-gender-diversity-initiatives-need-a-reboot

[24] https://execpipeline.com/wp-content/uploads/2021/07/Women-Count-2021-Report.pdf

Part 2: Cultural frameworks

[25] www.mckinsey.com/featured-insights/diversity-and-inclusion/women-in-the-workplace

[26] https://hbr.org/2019/06/research-women-score-higher-than-men-in-most-leadership-skills

27 www.theguardian.com/women-in-leadership/2013/nov/19/maria-miller-workplace-designed-for-men

28 www.bitc.org.uk/wp-content/uploads/2020/08/bitc-report-gender-ttt50supplement-july20.pdf

29 www.mckinsey.com/featured-insights/diversity-and-inclusion/women-in-the-workplace

30 www.managers.org.uk/knowledge-and-insights/research-thought-leadership/management-transformed/

31 www.dontfixwomen.com

32 www.dontfixwomen.com

33 https://www.managementtoday.co.uk/will-hybrid-working-ever-work/leadership-lessons/article/1696011

34 www.flexjobs.com/blog/post/survey-productivity-balance-improve-during-pandemic-remote-work/

35 www.employersforcarers.org/membership/business-case

36 https://www.theguardian.com/business/2022/jun/06/thousands-workers-worlds-biggest-trial-four-day-week

37 www.pwc.co.uk/press-room/press-releases/pwc-announces-new-flexible-work-deal.html

38 https://civilservice.blog.gov.uk/2019/06/14/happy-job-sharing-caring-fathers-day/

39 www.managementtoday.co.uk/job sharing-work/personal-development/article/1424603

40 https://link.springer.com/article/10.1007/s11205-018-2036-7

41 https://www.gov.uk/government/news/government-says-in-the-interest-of-employers-and-employees-to-make-offer-of-flexible-working-standard

42 https://civilservice.blog.gov.uk/2020/02/18/we-is-the-key-gender-equal-job-sharing-in-the-civil-service/

43 www.linkedin.com/pulse/new-survey-reveals-85-all-jobs-filled-via-networking-lou-adler/

44 https://wiw-report.s3.amazonaws.com/Women_in_the_Workplace_2018.pdf

[45] https://hbswk.hbs.edu/item/professional-networking-makes-people-feel-dirty

[46] www.lexico.com/definition/networking

[47] www.bcg.com/en-gb/publications/2017/people-organization-behavior-culture-five-ways-men-improve-gender-diversity-work

[48] David G. Smith and W. Brad Johnson, *Good Guys: How Men Can Be Better Allies for Women in the Workplace*, p. 7. 2020, Harvard Business Review Press.

[49] www.bbc.co.uk/news/education-55309923

[50] www.kcl.ac.uk/news/inequality-between-women-and-men-doesnt-really-exist-say-one-in-seven-britons

[51] www2.deloitte.com/global/en/pages/about-deloitte/articles/women-at-work-global-outlook.html

[52] https://www.forbes.com/sites/joyburnford/2021/05/26/men-the-missing-piece-of-the-gender-balance-jigsaw/?sh=60654fd25f4e

[53] www.everywoman.com/inclusion-action, p. 10.

[54] www.theguardian.com/sustainable-business/2016/jun/08/workplace-gender-equality-invisible-privilege

[55] https://static.store.tax.thomsonreuters.com/static/relatedresource/CMJ--15-01%20sample-article.pdf

[56] www.managers.org.uk/about-cmi/media-centre/press-office/press-releases/sponsorship-and-mentoring-crucial-to-increasing-gender-diversity-at-executive-level/

[57] https://podcasts.apple.com/us/podcast/the-power-of-coaching-and-mentoring-with-sian-prigg/id1569407791?i=1000527841404

[58] www.dontfixwomen.com

[59] https://30percentclub.org/news/

[60] https://ecommons.cornell.edu/bitstream/handle/1813/74541/What_Evidence_is_There_That_Mentoring_Works_to_Retain_and_Promote_Employees.pdf?sequence=1&isAllowed=y

[61] www.mckinsey.com/featured-insights/diversity-and-inclusion/women-in-the-workplace

[62] www2.deloitte.com/uk/en/pages/impact-report-2019/stories/reverse-mentoring.html

[63] https://hbr.org/2019/10/why-reverse-mentoring-works-and-how-to-do-it-right

[64] Institute of Leadership & Management Report, *Creating a coaching culture*, May 2011, p. 2.

[65] www.betterup.com/blog/coaching-gender-gap

[66] www.forbes.com/sites/forbescoachescouncil/2020/02/19/13-ways-business-owners-can-encourage-gender-equality-through-company-culture/?sh=4463bd8e2288

[67] Alison Hardingham, *The Coach's Coach: Personal Development for Personal Developers*, CIPD Kogan Page.

[68] https://coachingfederation.org/research/building-a-coaching-culture

[69] www.hbr.org/2021/02/research-men-get-more-actionable-feedback-than-women

[70] As heard on podcast www.cipd.co.uk/podcasts/coaching-culture

[71] www.institutelm.com/resourceLibrary/creating-a-coaching-culture-2011.html

[72] www.hrzone.com/community/blogs/gfreynolds/average-employee-costs-smes-ps11000-to-replace

[73] http://thehealthyexec.com/wp-content/uploads/2018/06/ICF-Global-Coaching-Client-Study-complete.pdf

[74] Sally Bonneywell, 'How a coaching intervention supports the development of female leaders in a global organisation', *International Journal of Evidence Based Coaching and Mentoring*, Special Issue No. 11, June 2017, p. 57.

[75] www.gsk.com/media/7458/2021-uk-gender-pay-gap-report.pdf

Part 3: Understanding the obstacles that women face at work

[76] www.mckinsey.com/featured-insights/diversity-and-inclusion/women-in-the-workplace

[77] www.managers.org.uk/about-cmi/media-centre/press-office/press-releases/too-many-women-at-the-bottom-still-not-enough-at-the-top/

[78] https://hellobonafide.com/pages/state-of-menopause

[79] https://workinmind.org/2021/12/07/the-menopause-at-work-designing-supportive-spaces/

[80] www.fawcettsociety.org.uk/Handlers/Download.ashx?IDMF=9672cf45-5f13-4b69-8882-1e5e643ac8a6

[81] https://committees.parliament.uk/writtenevidence/39340/html

[82] www.bloombergquint.com/business/women-are-leaving-the-workforce-for-a-little-talked-about-reason

[83] www.hrmagazine.co.uk/content/features/supporting-employees-through-the-menopause/

[84] www.fom.ac.uk/health-at-work-2/information-for-employers/dealing-with-health-problems-in-the-workplace/advice-on-the-menopause

[85] www.ons.gov.uk/peoplepopulationandcommunity/birthsdeathsandmarriages/lifeexpectancies/bulletins/nationallifetablesunitedkingdom/2018to2020#:~:text=1.,period%20of%202015%20to%202017

[86] www.peoplemanagement.co.uk/article/1751699/three-quarters-businesses-still-have-no-menopause-policy-study-finds

[87] www.peoplemanagement.co.uk/news/articles/number-tribunals-involving-menopause-triples-in-three-years-research-finds#gref

[88] www.managementtoday.co.uk/prevent-losing-female-leaders-menopause/women-in-business/article/1722900

[89] https://podcasts.apple.com/us/podcast/regain-control-of-your-hormones-with-nicki-williams/id1569407791?i=1000545478101

[90] www.womensmidlifehealthjournal.biomedcentral.com/articles/10.1186/s40695-022-00073-y

[91] www.wellbeingofwomen.org.uk/campaigns/menopausepledge/stories/our-aim-at-santander-is-to-normalise-discussion-about-the-menopause-at-work

[92] www.cipd.co.uk/about/media/press/menopause-at-work#gref

[93] www.wtw-healthandbenefits.co.uk/news/overhaul-of-employee-benefits

[94] www.wellbeingofwomen.org.uk/campaigns/menopausepledge

[95] https://twitter.com/jamestcobbler/status/1450001078297284609

96 www.mckinsey.com/featured-insights/diversity-and-inclusion/ten-things-to-know-about-gender-equality

97 www.bristol.ac.uk/news/2019/october/new-mums-careers.html

98 https://workplaceinsight.net/women-less-likely-to-progress-at-work-than-their-male-counterparts-following-childbirth/

99 www.citizensadvice.org.uk/work/rights-at-work/parental-rights/rights-while-youre-on-maternity-leave/

100 https://hbr.org/2020/07/why-wfh-isnt-necessarily-good-for-women

101 www.imperial.ac.uk/news/194715/miscarriage-ectopic-pregnancy-trigger-long-term-post-traumatic/

102 www.nytimes.com/2020/11/25/opinion/meghan-markle-miscarriage.html

103 https://fertilitynetworkuk.org/

104 https://fertilitynetworkuk.org/wp-content/uploads/2016/10/SURVEY-RESULTS-Impact-of-Fertility-Problems.pdf

105 www.jri.ir/article/30043

106 https://fertilitynetworkuk.org/survey-on-the-impact-of-fertility-problems/

107 www.thetimes.co.uk/article/babies-law-firm-fertility-officer-employment-equality-9f79jt6nv

108 https://colleagues.coop.co.uk/pregnancy-loss-policy

109 https://inews.co.uk/news/business/john-lewis-joins-companies-offering-time-off-for-pregnancy-loss-and-equalises-parental-leave-1044458

110 Emma Barnett, *It's About Bloody Time. Period*, HarperCollins Publishers, p. 112. Reprinted by permission of HarperCollins Publishers Ltd © Emma Barnett 2019.

111 www.devex.com/news/menstruationmatters-to-all-not-just-girls-88221

112 https://qz.com/611774/period-pain-can-be-as-bad-as-a-heart-attack-so-why-arent-we-researching-how-to-treat-it/

113 www.bloodygoodperiod.com/employers-research

114 https://edition.cnn.com/2016/02/16/asia/china-menstruation-leave/index.html

115 www.bbc.com/news/world-europe-61429022.amp

116 www.theguardian.com/lifeandstyle/2016/mar/04/period-policy-asia-menstrual-leave-japan-women-work

117 www.zomato.com/blog/period-leaves

118 www.rcn.org.uk/clinical-topics/womens-health/endometriosis

119 www.bloodygoodperiod.com/employers-research

120 https://assets.publishing.service.gov.uk/government/uploads/system/uploads/attachment_data/file/840404/KCL_Main_Report.pdf

121 www.dontfixwomen.com

122 www.ipsos.com/en-uk/who-cares-business-community-ipsos-research-reveals-great-workplace-divide

123 www.theguardian.com/world/2022/mar/31/almost-half-of-working-age-women-in-uk-do-45-hours-of-unpaid-care-a-week-study

124 www.fom.ac.uk/health-at-work-2/information-for-employers/dealing-with-health-problems-in-the-workplace/advice-on-the-menopause

125 www.ipsos.com/en-uk/who-cares-business-community-ipsos-research-reveals-great-workplace-divide

126 www.bitc.org.uk/wp-content/uploads/2020/08/bitc-report-gender-ttt50supplement-july20.pdf

127 www.carersuk.org/news-and-campaigns/press-releases/employers-more-supportive-of-caring-but-carers-still-at-risk-of-leaving-work-unless-more-measures-adopted

128 Eve Rodsky, *Fair Play: Share the Mental Load, Rebalance Your Relationship and Transform Your Life*, Quercus.

129 www.mckinsey.com/featured-insights/diversity-and-inclusion/women-in-the-workplace

130 https://pregnantthenscrewed.com/one-in-four-parents-say-that-they-have-had-to-cut-down-on-heat-food-clothing-to-pay-for-childcare/

131 https://ifs.org.uk/uploads/BN290-Mothers-and-fathers-balancing-work-and-life-under-lockdown.pdf

132 Ed Miliband, *Go Big: How to Fix Our World*, Penguin Vintage, p. 60.

133 https://link.springer.com/book/10.1007%2F978-3-319-42970-0

134 www.theguardian.com/lifeandstyle/2014/jun/15/fathers-spend-more-time-with-children-than-in-1970s

135 https://promundoglobal.org/wp-content/uploads/2019/06/
BLS19063_PRO_SOWF_REPORT_015.pdf

136 www.weforum.org/agenda/2016/08/these-10-countries-have-the-
best-parental-leave-policies-in-the-world

137 www.unicef-irc.org/family-friendly

138 https://sweden.se/life/society/work-life-balance

139 www.bi.team/wp-content/uploads/2021/06/PI-dual-trial-report-
080621-for-upload.pdf

140 https://news.gallup.com/businessjournal/196058/
kids-company-greatest-competition.aspx?g_source=CATEGORY_
WOMENS_ISSUES&g_medium=topic&g_campaign=tiles

141 www.mckinsey.com/featured-insights/diversity-and-inclusion/
women-in-the-workplace

142 www.tsb.co.uk/news-releases/tsb-pledges-equal-parental-leave/

143 www.bbc.co.uk/news/business-60328314

144 http://social-policy.org.uk/wordpress/wp-content/uploads/2015/04/
22_naumann.pdf

145 www.carersuk.org/images/CarersWeek2020/CW_2020_Research_
Report_WEB.pdf

146 www.carersuk.org/images/News_and_campaigns/Juggling_work_
and_unpaid_care_report_final_0119_WEB.pdf

147 www.cipd.co.uk/Images/supporting-working-carers-2_
tcm18-80339.pdf

148 www.bitc.org.uk/wp-content/uploads/2020/08/bitc-report-
gender-ttt50supplement-july20.pdf

149 www.carersuk.org/for-professionals/policy/policy-library/
facts-about-carers-2019

150 www.carersuk.org/images/News__campaigns/CarersRightsDay_
Nov19_FINAL.pdf

151 www.carersuk.org/images/News_and_campaigns/Carers_Rights_
Day/CRD_2021/Carers_Rights_Day_report_2021.pdf

152 www.employersforcarers.org/files/pdfs/Who_Cares_Wins.pdf

153 www.carersuk.org/images/News_and_campaigns/Carers_Rights_
Day/CRD_2021/Carers_Rights_Day_report_2021.pdf

154 www.cipd.co.uk/Images/supporting-working-carers-2_
tcm18-80339.pdf

155 https://careers.aviva.co.uk/working-at-aviva/

156 www.carersuk.org/images/News_and_campaigns/Carers_Rights_
Day/CRD_2021/Carers_Rights_Day_report_2021.pdf

157 www.employersforcarers.org

158 Employer for Carers@ www.employersforcarers.org/ and Jointly:
https://jointlyapp.com/

159 www.carerspassports.uk

160 www.carersuk.org/news-and-campaigns/press-release-rss/4761-
7-in-10-people-juggling-their-job-with-caring-for-a-loved-one-feel-
isolated-at-work

161 www.forbes.com/sites/tamiforman/2017/12/13/self-care-is-not-
an-indulgence-its-a-discipline/?sh=1600fa85fee0

162 www2.deloitte.com/global/en/pages/about-deloitte/articles/
women-at-work-global-outlook.html

163 www.who.int/news/item/28-05-2019-burn-out-an-occupational-
phenomenon-international-classification-of-diseases

164 Speech delivered by Bryan Dyson at the 172nd commencement of
the Georgia Tech Institute, on 6 September 1996.

165 www.bbc.com/worklife/article/20210518-the-hidden-load-how-
thinking-of-everything-holds-mums-back

166 https://employeebenefits.co.uk/organon-gives-staff-day-off-
international-womens-day/

167 www.dontfixwomen.com

168 www.thefemalelead.com/post/close-the-entitlementgap-with-the-
female-lead

169 Louisa Jewell, *Wire Your Brain for Confidence: The Science of Conquering
Self-Doubt*, Famous Warrior Press, p. 99.

170 www.dontfixwomen.com

171 www.ft.com/content/80718674-ef38-11e9-a55a-30afa498db1b

172 www.allgreatquotes.com/quote-377122/

173 www.bbc.co.uk/news/world-41097043

Part 4: Navigate your route

[174] https://execpipeline.com/wp-content/uploads/2021/07/Women-Count-2021-Report.pdf

[175] Marc Benioff and Monica Langley, *Trailblazer: The Power of Business as the Greatest Platform for Change*, Simon & Schuster, p. 119.

List of Figures

Figure 1: Why gender equality is a business imperative

- US$28 trillion added to global GDP: www.mckinsey.com/featured-insights/diversity-and-inclusion/ten-things-to-know-about-gender-equality
- 25% more likely to have above-average profitability: www.mckinsey.com/featured-insights/diversity-andinclusion/diversity-wins-how-inclusion-matters
- £123 billion lost in pre-tax profits: https://execpipeline.com/wp-content/uploads/2021/07/Women-Count-2021-Report.pdf
- 3 x higher profit margins: www.execpipeline.com/wp-content/uploads/2019/07/the-pipeline-womencount-2019.pdf
- 19% higher innovation revenue: www.bcg.com/en-us/publications/2018/how-diverse-leadership-teams-boost-innovation
- 61% of women look at diversity of employers: www.pwc.com/gx/en/about/diversity/iwd/iwd-female-talent-report-web.pdf

Figure 2: The Gender Allies Matrix™

Figure 3: SPACES™ Framework

Figure 4: Menopause statistics

- 99% say their symptoms negatively impacted their work: https://balance-website-prod.s3-eu-west-1.amazonaws.com/uploads/2021/10/Menopause-and-work-poster-RCGP.pdf
- 59% have taken time off work due to their symptoms: https://balance-website-prod.s3-eu-west-1.amazonaws.com/uploads/2021/10/Menopause-and-work-poster-RCGP.pdf

- ⓔ 42% have considered leaving their job due to the menopause: www.lattelounge.co.uk/42-of-women-consider-leaving-job-due-to-menopause/
- ⓔ 50% feel there is a stigma around talking about the menopause: www.vodafone.com/news/press-release/vodafone-announces-new-global-employee-commitment-menopause
- ⓔ 84% say there is no workplace support, or they are unsure that it exists: www.lattelounge.co.uk/42-of-women-consider-leaving-job-due-to-menopause/
- ⓔ 4.5 million working women are in the 50–64 age bracket, the fastest-growing, economically active group: https://committees.parliament.uk/writtenevidence/39340/html/

Figure 5: Maternity statistics

- ⓔ Fewer than 1 in 5 of all new mothers follow a full-time career after maternity leave: https://assets.publishing.service.gov.uk/government/uploads/system/uploads/attachment_data/file/840062/Bristol_Final_Report_1610.pdf
- ⓔ Only 31% of mothers return to, and remain in, full-time work five years after birth: https://assets.publishing.service.gov.uk/government/uploads/system/uploads/attachment_data/file/840062/Bristol_Final_Report_1610.pdf
- ⓔ 90% of men remain either in full-time work or self-employed in the 3 years after birth: https://assets.publishing.service.gov.uk/government/uploads/system/uploads/attachment_data/file/840062/Bristol_Final_Report_1610.pdf
- ⓔ 21% of women are nervous to tell their boss they are pregnant: www.brighthorizons.com/newsroom/modern-family-index-2018
- ⓔ 65% of women without children worry about what having a child will mean for their career: www.brighthorizons.com/newsroom/modern-family-index-2018
- ⓔ 69% say working mothers are more likely to be passed up for a new job than other employees: www.brighthorizons.com/newsroom/modern-family-index-2018

Figure 6: Miscarriage statistics

ⓔ 1 in 4 pregnancies end in miscarriage: www.tommys.org/
pregnancy-information/im-pregnant/early-pregnancy/
how-common-miscarriage

ⓔ 85% of miscarriages happen in the first 12 weeks of
pregnancy: www.tommys.org/pregnancy-information/
im-pregnant/early-pregnancy/how-common-miscarriage

ⓔ 23 million miscarriages occur every year worldwide: www.
tommys.org/baby-loss-support/miscarriage-information-
and-support/miscarriage-statistics#second-trimester

ⓔ 1 in 100 women experience recurrent miscarriages (3 or
more in a row): www.tommys.org/baby-loss-support/
miscarriage-information-and-support/miscarriage-statistics#
second-trimester

ⓔ 29% of women experience long-term post-traumatic stress
following miscarriage: www.imperial.ac.uk/news/194715/
miscarriage-ectopic-pregnancy-trigger-long-term-post-
traumatic/

ⓔ 24% of women experience moderate to severe anxiety
following miscarriage: www.imperial.ac.uk/news/194715/
miscarriage-ectopic-pregnancy-trigger-long-term-post-
traumatic/

Figure 7: Monthlies statistics

ⓔ More than 800 million girls and women between the ages of
15 and 49 are menstruating on any given day: www.fsg.org/
blog/menstrual-health-and-gender-equity

ⓔ 1 in 5 women find painful menstruation (dysmenorrhea)
interferes with their daily life: www.aafp.org/afp/2012/0215/
p386.html

ⓔ Over 5 million sick days each year are taken by women
suffering from heavy periods: www.aafp.org/afp/2012/0215/
p386.html

ⓔ £531 million: cost to the British economy of sick days taken
related to heavy periods: www.independent.
co.uk/life-style/health-and-families/

heavy-periods-sick-days-five-million-uk-economy-
menorrhagia-a8000131.html?amp

◎ 46% of women aren't comfortable talking about their period
as a reason for time off work: www.bupa.co.uk/business/
news-and-information/female-health-and-employment

◎ 67% of women agreed they would be more honest about their
symptoms with a female boss: www.bupa.co.uk/business/
news-and-information/female-health-and-employment

Figure 8: Childcare statistics

◎ 43% of mums say that the cost of childcare has made them
consider leaving their job, and 40% say they have had to
work fewer hours because of childcare costs: https://
pregnantthenscrewed.com/one-in-four-parents-say-that-they-have-
had-to-cut-down-on-heat-food-clothing-to-pay-for-childcare/

◎ 72% of both working mums and dads agree that women
are penalized in their careers for starting families, while
men are not: www.brighthorizons.com/-/media/BH-New/
Newsroom/Media-Kit/MFI_2018_Report_FINAL.ashx

◎ Only 2% of eligible couples make use of shared parental
leave: www.emwllp.com/latest/shared-parental-leave-in-
crease/

◎ 1 in 7 workers have to make significant changes to their work
pattern to balance work, childcare and home-schooling: www.
icaew.com/insights/viewpoints-on-the-news/2020/aug-2020/
the-new-normal-of-employment-rights-and-childcare

◎ 28% of women with school-age children left the workforce to
become a primary caregiver to children during the pandemic,
compared to 10% of men: https://time.com/nextadvisor/
in-the-news/women-in-the-workplace/

◎ 73% of mums believe they get fewer career advancement
opportunities than women who are not mothers:
www.brighthorizons.com/-/media/BH-New/Newsroom/
Media-Kit/MFI_2018_Report_FINAL.ashx

Figure 9: Eldercare statistics

ⓔ Statistics taken from: www.cipd.co.uk/Images/supporting-working-carers-2_tcm18-80339.pdf

Figure 10: Wellbeing and self-care statistics

ⓔ 72% of employees rated wellbeing as the top priority for 2021: www.managers.org.uk/knowledge-and-insights/research-thought-leadership/management-transformed/

ⓔ 75% of UK workers reported suffering with burnout in 2020: https://blog.asana.com/2021/01/uk-anatomy-of-work-infographic/

ⓔ 2x: the gap in burnout between women and men has almost doubled: www.mckinsey.com/featured-insights/diversity-and-inclusion/women-in-the-workplace

ⓔ 55% of working carers feel overwhelmed by their caring role: www.carersweek.org/media/u4jby32a/carers-week-2021-research-report.pdf

ⓔ 75% of working carers feel exhausted as a result of their caring role: www.carersweek.org/media/u4jby32a/carers-week-2021-research-report.pdf

ⓔ 71% of working carers feel stressed and anxious as a result of caring: www.carersweek.org/media/u4jby32a/carers-week-2021-research-report.pdf

Figure 11: Confidence at work statistics

ⓔ Statistics taken from: www.dontfixwomen.com

Index